design ideas for Home Landscaping

Catriona Tudor Erler

CREATIVE HOMEOWNER®, Upper Saddle River, New Jersey

CREATIVE
HOMEOWNER®

A Division of Federal Marketing Corp.
Upper Saddle River, NJ

DESIGN IDEAS FOR HOME LANDSCAPING

SENIOR EDITOR	Kathie Robitz
EDITOR	Lisa Kahn
SENIOR GRAPHIC DESIGN COORDINATOR	Glee Barre
PHOTO RESEARCHER	Robyn Poplasky
EDITORIAL ASSISTANT	Jennifer Calvert and Nora Grace
INDEXER	Schroeder Indexing Services
COVER DESIGN	Glee Barre
ALL COVER PHOTOGRAPHY	Catriona Tudor Erler
ILLUSTRATIONS	Clarke Barre: pages 130–131 Catriona Tudor Erler: pages 25, 88 Nancy Hull: pages 19, 27, 144–155, 153, 159

CREATIVE HOMEOWNER

VICE PRESIDENT AND PUBLISHER	Timothy O. Bakke
PRODUCTION DIRECTOR	Kimberly H. Vivas
ART DIRECTOR	David Geer
MANAGING EDITOR	Fran J. Donegan

Current Printing (last digit)
10 9 8 7 6 5 4 3 2 1

Design Ideas for Home Landscaping, First Edition
Library of Congress Control Number: 2007922559
ISBN-10: 1-58011-371-0
ISBN-13: 978-1-58011-371-7
CREATIVE HOMEOWNER®
A Division of Federal Marketing Corp.
24 Park Way
Upper Saddle River, NJ 07458
www.creativehomeowner.com

Dedication

To my husband, Jim, who gave willingly of his time and expertise to process the photographs.

Acknowledgments

Producing a book requires many behind-the-scenes people who are essential to the success of the final product. I'd like to thank my editor Lisa Kahn and senior designer Glee Barre for the great job they did integrating my words and pictures into a compelling book, and for their encouraging support through the writing process. I am also grateful to Tim Bakke and Kathie Robitz for asking me to write this book for Creative Homeowner.

A host of people have opened their homes and gardens to me to photograph their private domains. A special thank you to the following people for their generous, gracious hospitality: Peter and Betsy Agelasto, Mark and Kathe Albrecht, John and Laura Alioto, James and Rebecca Allen, Patrick Anderson, Allison Armour-Wilson (Baldhorns Park), Lyle Arnold, Maria Baker, Debra Baldwin, Robert Bell, Brian and Mimi Benjamin, Dan and Parkie Blaylock, John Brookes (Denmans Garden), Norie Burnet, Don Buser, Edward and Terry Carr, Leigh and Brenda Chisholm, Scott and Mary Clifton, Laurie Connable, Roger Cornell, Phil and Ann Crowley, Jeff and Patty Daniels, Terry and Courtnay Daniels (Whilton Farm), Alec and Sarah Don, Gavin and Belinda Don, Hudson and Mary Drake, Theodore and Adrian Erler, Patty Finch, Bill Frederick, Lani Freymiller, Anne Gilliam, Erik and Irina Gronborg, Leila Grossinger, John Grzebian, Wallace Gusler, Joe and Susannah Haber, Ed and Ada Harvey, Stephen Haus, Don Haynie and Tom Hamlin (Buffalo Springs Herb Farm), Thomas Helm, Rob and Debbie Hewell, Michael and Caroline Hill, Kate Hofstetter, Harry and Mary Ellen Hunt, Bob and Joyce Johnson, Jeffrey and Marci Krinsk, Inta Krombolz, John and Carol Landis, Linda Lear and John Nickum, Ann Lederer, Calder Loth, Betty Mackie, Alex and Susan Mandl, Patricia Smith Melton, Allen Mushinsk, Cheryl Nogle, Alex and Libbey Oliver, Jerry and Janet Potter, John and Barbara Quarles, F. Turner and Nancy Reuter, Zandra Rhodes, Alfred and Bridgett Ritter, Patricia Rinaker, Glenn and Pam Rosenthal, Scott Rothenberger, William and Sukey Roxburgh, David and Phoebe Sackett, Osamu and Holly Shimizu, Connie Slack, John and Sumako Solenberger, John and Mary Lew Sponski (Tre Sorelle), Lucy Sydnor (Dancing Point), Phil and Gayle Tauber, Bernard and Carol Tautkus, Per and Eve Thyrum, Jack Todd, Juan and Susi Torre-Bueno, Gordon and Lisa Tudor, Diane Uke, Ted and Katie Ukrop, Nicholas Wallner, John and Mary Walsh, Peter and Louise Warne (Frith Hill), Margot Washburn, Phillip Watson, Evelyn Weidner, Pat Welsh, Penny West, Mary Sherman Willis, Michael and Audrey Wyatt, and Agatha Youngblood.

A special thank you also to Mark Oxley of Outdoor Illumination, Inc., who introduced me to some stunning gardens and taught me so much about the principles of outdoor lighting. I also appreciate his willingness to allow me to use his colleague Karen Weaver's lighting design. (Page 88.) H. Clay Johnston of Outdoor Lighting Perspectives of Central & Southern Virginia also has my gratitude for introducing me to the Hunts' garden on Smith Mountain Lake.

Finally, a big hug and many, many thanks to my husband, Jim, for his technical help and his emotional support while I was writing this book. I couldn't have done it without him.

Contents

Introduction 6

Chapter 1
Start with a Plan 9
- principles of design
- gathering information
- devising your scheme

Chapter 2
Garden Styles 32
- international styles
- three centuries of american design
- american regional traditions

Chapter 3
Outdoor Living Space 64
- defining your space
- clever garden rooms
- family-friendly play areas
- outdoor dining
- secret retreats
- front gardens

Chapter 4
Let There Be Light 80
- the well-lit garden
- developing a scheme
- lighting options

Chapter 5
Featuring Plants 94
- garden compositions
- color-themed gardens
- living walls and partitions
- charming topiaries
- knot gardens
- plants for drama
- vegetable gardens

Chapter 6
Accent on the Garden 110
- structural statements
- garden pathways
- special touches
- water features
- in and out of sight
- places to perch

Chapter 7
Garden Habitats 164
- lofty elevations
- humid climates
- wooded locales
- urban and desert oases

Chapter 8
Seasonal Gardens 188
- nature's rhythms
- spring awakening
- summer blooms
- autumn color
- winter landscapes

Resource Guide 198

Glossary 200

Index 204

ABOVE Zen gardens are restful places, ideal for contemplation. A commercial project designed by Julie Moir Messervy inspired this scaled-down residential version.

RIGHT A mosaic of broken tiles covers the fluid curves of this fanciful wall, while a pink clematis climbs its face.

BELOW A gazing globe creates a compelling focal point and an unexpected perspective on the garden.

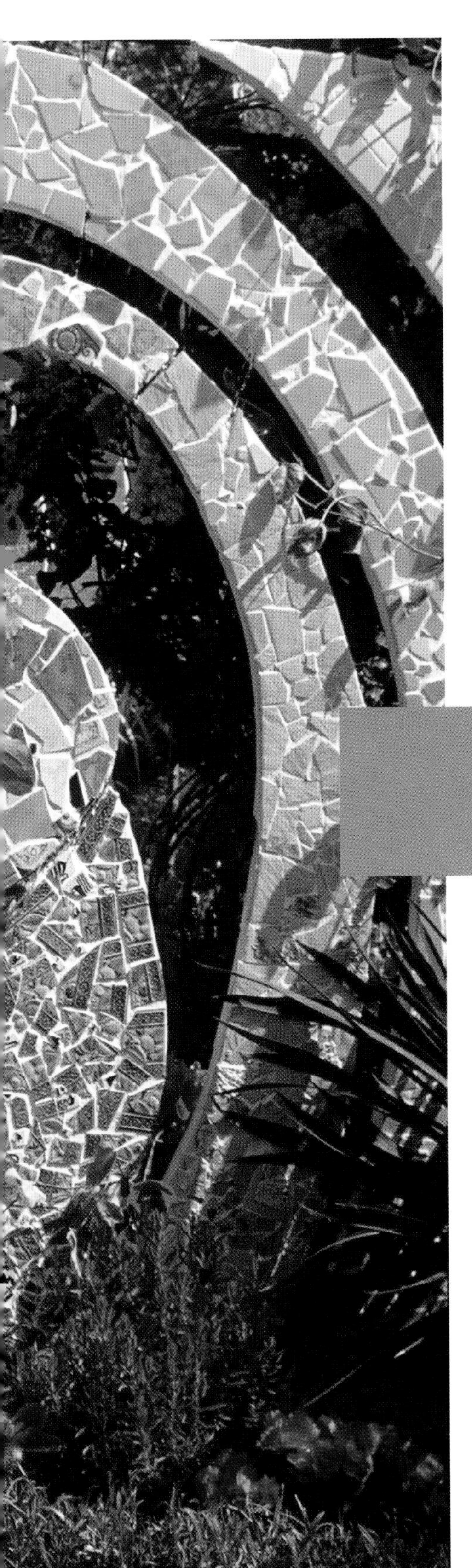

Introduction

Landscaping is a creative endeavor, a journey full of possibilities, and an adventure. You are faced with scores of garden-design traditions that hail from different regions of the country and every corner of the world, as well as thousands of plants, with dozens of new varieties introduced every year. There are also countless options for paving, fencing, and other architectural details. They range from organic materials, such as wood and stone, to the very latest synthetic products. In addition, your family may have many different uses in mind for the outdoor space. The children may clamor for a play area, the adults, a private spa or water feature. Someone may be hankering for a vegetable garden, an outdoor kitchen, or a spot for alfresco dining and entertaining. So where does one begin when faced with so many choices?

Whether you are starting from scratch or altering an existing scheme, *Design Ideas for Home Landscaping* will give you perspective and inspire you with hundreds of ideas for making your garden just what you want it to be. As you look through the photographs, focus on specific details, such as plant combinations or fencing styles, that you can adapt to your own space. For example, if a large garden appeals to you, but you only have a tiny city lot, remember that the scale can be altered and details changed to fit your unique space.

Enjoy the beautiful landscape designs on these pages, and let them motivate you to explore the many possibilities for your own garden.

ABOVE The gentle curve of these dry-laid stone stairs makes them more interesting than a straight flight.

RIGHT The trellis arch is a vertical focal point, framing the path and central container.

1

Before you plant a single tree or shrub, it is a good idea to have a cohesive master plan from which you or a professional landscape designer can work. You can create the plan yourself or hire a professional to do it. Whether you intend to finish your entire landscape all at once or work on it a section at a time over many years, this plan will be a useful guide. An understanding of basic design concepts is invaluable for developing a successful design that has singleness of thought, and is visually pleasing, harmonious, and exciting.

Start with a Plan

- principles of design
- gathering information
- devising your scheme

Good garden design begins with a plan for paths, beds, lawns, hedges, and other features. You can implement the plan at once or in stages, depending on your budget.

Harmony and unity; proportion and scale; light and shade; mass and space; texture, pattern, and color: all are aspects of a successful landscape design. When effectively used, they are valuable tools to serve the designer's visual goals.

Time is the one element that gardeners, unlike artists, must handle. A garden is always growing and changing. One day a flower may be in bud, the next in bloom, and a week later, the display is spent. In the early years after it is first planted, a tree or shrub may be too small for its setting, needing several growing seasons to reach its full potential. Over time, plants age and die. The dimension of time and the changes it brings is an extra challenge to a garden designer, but the dynamics of working with things that are alive and ever-changing is also part of the joy of making a garden.

Truly great gardens incorporate the design principles discussed here, as well as the evolving appearance of the plants, to create delightful tensions between restfulness and stimulation. They are harmonious without being repetitive and boring. These well-designed gardens are balanced and unified, and at the same time surprising.

principles of design

ABOVE This small gazebo is beautifully in scale with the pocket-size seaside garden. The structure's built-in benches provide ample seating space without taking up too much room.

RIGHT This deep purple and black color combination is created with sweet potato vine 'Blackie', a deep-blue flowering verbena, and the purple and silver leaves of Persian shield. To look their best, these dramatic colors need the background of silvery artemisia. The white flower buds of the sedum 'Autumn Joy' will turn pink and then rusty red as the season progresses.

OPPOSITE Spiky-yellow verbascum flowers contrast with globe-shape purple allium and yellow tulips. The design is rich with texture, color, a balance of mass and space, and proportion and scale.

harmony and unity

Here are some ideas for creating a harmonious, unified landscape design:

- **Develop a Concept**
  Well-balanced gardens have a clear sense of purpose and intent. Choose a style and be consistent with it.
- **Connect to the Setting**
  The overall garden should coordinate with the style of the house.
  If you have views beyond the garden, relate your landscape to the local terrain by growing native plants, using indigenous rock, or echoing a dominant shape, color, or form from the view outside the garden.
- **Keep Plants in Balance**
  Grow plants together that have similar needs. It is jarring to see plants that require plenty of water growing next to those that prefer dry conditions.
  Shape plants sympathetically. Clipped yews, hollies, and boxwoods are more appropriate for a formal design. In a woodland garden, those same plants look more harmonious if allowed to grow in their natural form.
- **Repetition and Rhythm**
  Repeat patterns and shapes of plants, paving styles, or other elements that mirror an architectural feature of the house.

LEFT With its free-form shape and black-painted bottom, this swimming pool resembles a natural pond in the woods and is in harmony with its setting.

RIGHT A satisfying rhythm of repeating forms is created by this avenue of pencil cedars (*Juniperus virginiana*). Throughout the day, the changing shadows of the trees add another pattern to the design.

BOTTOM This landscape harmonizes well with the borrowed view of the fields and meadow.

bright idea

repetition

Repeat a color or planting to enhance a sense of unity.

Proportion and scale refer to the size, location, or amount of one item in a setting compared with another. When proportions are in balance, the garden looks right. Even in a pint-size garden, provide some sense of bulk and stature with a vertical element such as a tree or trellis to draw the eye away from the close boundaries of the property.

proportion and scale

TOP LEFT For pleasing proportions, designers recommend that the depth of a border be at least two-thirds the height of the structure or hedge behind it. For example, a border planted in front of a 6-ft.-tall hedge should be at least 4 ft. deep, measurements very close to the proportions in Fibonacci's number series (4:6 = 2:3). For foundation plantings, the bed depth should be about as wide as the height of the tallest shrub in the bed.

TOP RIGHT Even though this garden room is tiny, the gray curry plant (*Helichrysum italicum*) in the center is fairly bulky, keeping the garden from feeling too small. The rounded shrubs echo the shape of the nearby tree canopy, adding another dimension to the design.

the fibonacci sequence

In 1202, Italian mathematician Leonardo Fibonacci discovered a series of numbers that are a ratio for pleasing proportions. The sequence is created by adding together the two numbers that precede the next (1 plus 2 is 3; 2 plus 3 is 5; 3 plus 5 is 8; et cetera). Thus, a well-proportioned garden room would be 8 x 13 ft., or any combination that fits the formula. Interestingly, this mathematical series closely matches the natural growth patterns of many plants, including the seed arrangement of a ripe sunflower.

RIGHT The dappled light under this wisteria-covered pergola paints moving patterns on the paving, a pleasing contrast to the bright sunshine in the rest of the garden. Use pattern created by shade to add movement to your garden. Plant an evenly spaced row of straight-trunk trees, and enjoy the stripes of shade that move across the ground as the sun arcs through the sky. Trees with high, light canopies cast a delightful dappled pattern that migrates as the day progresses.

BELOW Color and light were explored time and again by the Impressionists. Claude Monet's painting, "The Garden, Giverny," shows how the interplay of color, light, and shadow affects the overall mood of the landscape. A good way to get inspiration for your own landscape design is to study some of these masterpieces.

light and shadow

The quality and intensity of light in your garden affects floral color. Because sun fades color, many flowers will appear to be brighter in a slightly shaded spot than in full sun. Also, the quality of light in various parts of the country affects how colors look. That's why tropical flowers look right in their native habitat but can sometimes be garish in other climates. The equatorial sun tones down the colors that can scream in softer northern lights.

You can also use light and shade for contrast in your garden. In a sunny garden, plant a spreading shade tree or build a structure that adds visual variety and provides some relief from the sun. Similarly, in a shady garden, open up an area to create a sunny oasis.

mass and space

An ideal design should contain a pleasing mix of bulk and space. Too much mass will make the garden appear heavy; too much horizontal space will make the garden look empty. Large, solid plants have mass, especially if their color is dark. Visually and physically, they help define and fill space, giving form to a design. Horizontal breaks, such as an expanse of patio, a reflecting pool, or a lawn, are visual resting places that are pleasing counterpoints to busier areas in the garden.

RIGHT The bulk of the boxwood provides a necessary anchor to the loose collection of plants in this composition.

BELOW The pond acts as negative space, giving the eye a place to rest and creating a pleasant contrast to the mounds of shrubs around its rim.

patterns

using landscape patterns

Dynamic Designs
The designs at right draw the eye across the space with the use of diagonal or zigzag lines, creating a sense of movement.

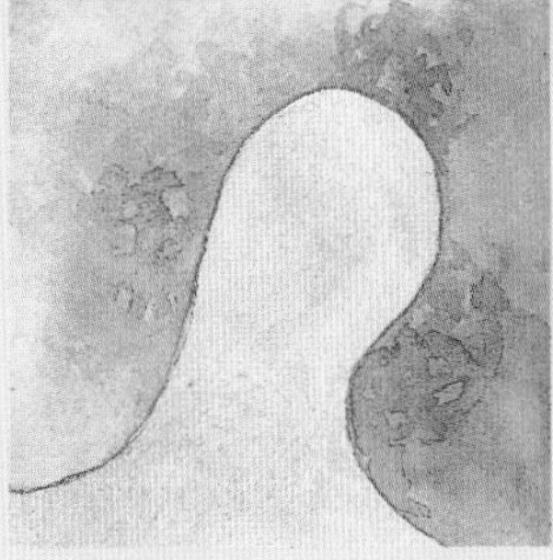
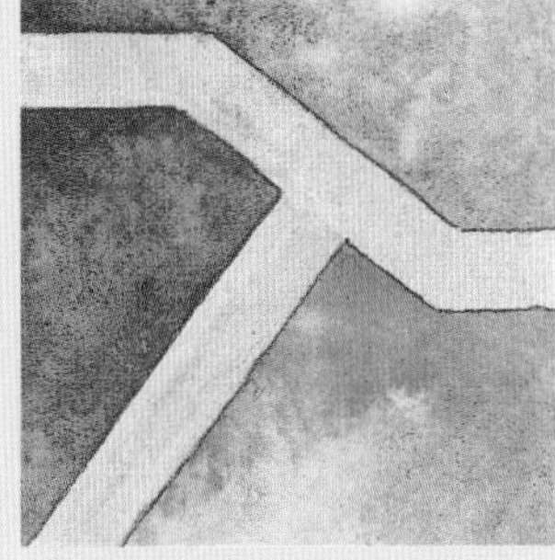
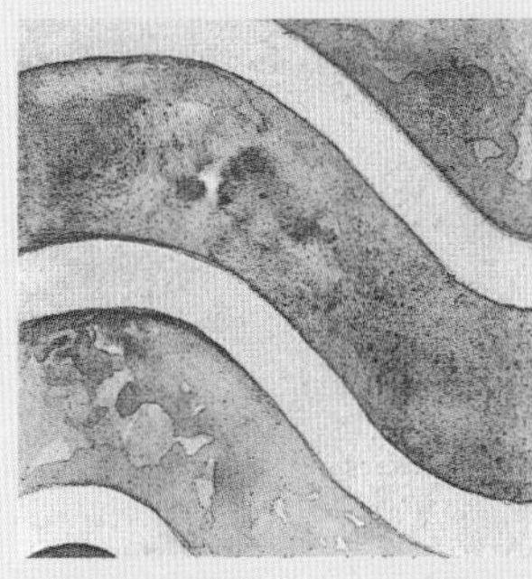

Static Designs
The pattern of these three garden designs is static, drawing attention to the center of the plan, rather than encouraging the eye to roam outside the space.

LEFT From an upstairs window, the spiral pattern of the azaleas is readily apparent. From the ground, visitors are drawn by the mystery of the curving path, screening what's just around the bend until the path opens up in the center to reveal the sculpture.

Garden patterns are formed by both the physical layout and plantings and by features such as paving. A repeating pattern, like the recurrent motif in a musical composition, helps give coherence to a garden design. The pattern may be geometric and symmetrical, typical in formal gardens, or a repeating free-form shape. Patterns also create a sense of movement or stability in a design. Diagonal lines and zigzags give an urgent sense of flow and draw the eye outward; a pattern that leads the eye to a central point will be more restful and static.

using textures for visual variety

Texture is the surface quality that can be seen and felt. It can be rough or smooth, soft or hard. Large-leaved plants are bold in texture, creating a strong, assertive impression. Small-leaved plants tend to have a delicate look. Too much of either will probably make a less-successful design than a balanced blend.

The shape of a plant also contributes to its texture and can influence your emotional response to the scene. Shrubs or flowers that reach boldly upward in a spike or spire add drama and even a spiritual boost to the design. In contrast, rounded shapes tend to be earthbound. Flat-headed flowers and trees and shrubs that branch out sideways are a horizontal element in a design, imparting an air of settled strength. Experiment with different effects by combining contrasting textures.

TOP LEFT The combination of 'Tiger Eye' sumac, red barberry, and hardy ageratum makes a rich textural composition.

TOP RIGHT The mosaic pebble paving introduces both pattern and texture to Oregon's Portland Classical Chinese Garden.

LEFT The bold leaves of oak-leaf hydrangea 'PeeWee' contrast pleasingly with the sedum flower buds.

OPPOSITE Purple-pink globes of *Allium aflatunense* juxtaposed with the yellow laburnum blossoms and lavender wisteria create an exciting visual relationship.

LEFT The yellow yarrow (*Achillea*) flowers combined with the deep-purple foliage of the smoke tree (*Cotinus coggyria purpureus*) produces a complementary combination of colors opposite each other on the color wheel.

OPPOSITE TOP The blue urn planted with a lotus echoes the tile color of the two walls.

OPPOSITE BOTTOM LEFT The salmon colors in *Agastache x rupestris*, *Coleus* 'Sedona', and a Phormium tenax hybrid form a monochromatic composition.

OPPOSITE BOTTOM RIGHT The white of the freeway daisies (*Osteospermum fruticosum*) adds sparkle to the deep-purple heliotrope flowers.

putting color to work

Beyond its intrinsic beauty, color is a valuable tool that can be used to create a sense of space or intimacy in your garden, to draw or deflect the eye, and to set a mood.

Colors react both to each other and to light, so how a color looks in the garden will depend on whether the planting is in sun or shade and what colors you put beside each other. Pastels stand out in soft light or shade but tend to look washed out in bright sun; strong colors hold their own in bright sun but may seem too extreme in a dimmer setting.

How you combine colors also affects their appearance and your response to them. Put together blue and orange, two colors opposite each other on the color wheel, and you've got a dynamic, vivid scene. Put the same blue next to purple for an analogous combination, and the picture will be much more muted. Use white to add sparkle to a composition, but avoid creating large patches of white among other colors, as it tends to visually punch a hole in your composition. Gray is a great connector, toning down combinations that might otherwise be too strong.

You can use color to manipulate the visual perception of space. Cool colors, such as blues, lilacs, and greens, tend to visually lengthen perceived distance. Reds, yellows, and oranges jump forward, with a foreshortening effect.

Colors evoke an emotional response in people. Blue is calming, red is exciting, sunny yellow lifts the spirits, and greens connect us with our origins.

color kinships

A color wheel helps us understand how colors relate in combination with each other.

- **Monochromatic relationships:** Combining colors that are variations of the same hue.
- **Analogous relationships:** Combining colors that are located adjacent to each other on a color wheel.
- **Complementary relationships:** Combining colors opposite each other on the color wheel.
- **Triad Relationship:** Three hues equally positioned on a color wheel.
- **Double-Complementary Relationship:** Two complementary-color combinations.

A site analysis is a thorough inventory of the topography and features on your property. These may include significant slopes or hills, structures, large trees, utility easements, and equipment such as air-conditioner units. A detailed analysis will also record any aesthetic factors, including attractive or unsightly views, and information on conditions that affect plant growth, such as wind patterns, warm or cold microclimates, and low spots where water may settle. Record this information on a base map, drawn to scale. (See the opposite page.) Armed with this knowledge, you'll be well equipped to care for your property over the years and to select the right plants and design elements.

gathering information

ABOVE By knowing where drainage is a problem on your property, you can resolve the issue with a dry streambed that channels water runoff.

LEFT Recording all the features of your garden on a site map gives you a good overview of what you have and may inspire ideas for changes you want to make.

BELOW Measuring your property is easier if you use a flexible, hand-winding measuring tape that is long enough to stretch the full length of your garden. Typically, retractable measuring tapes are not long enough for landscape dimensions, and they can be ruined if you get dirt in the winding mechanism.

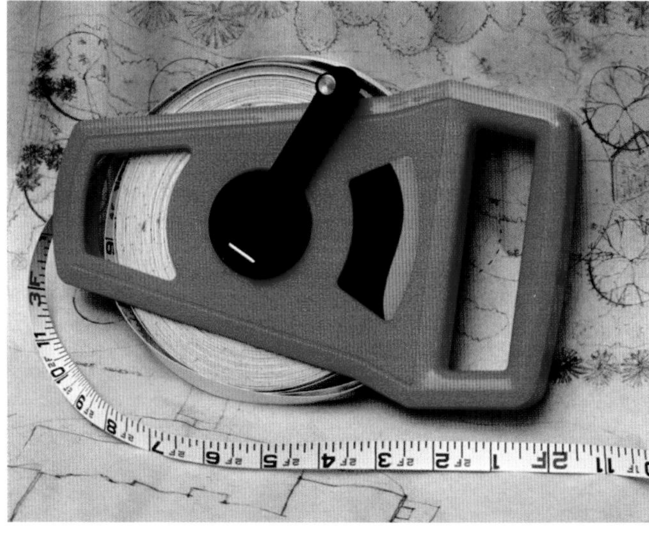

begin with a **b**ase **m**ap

You can create a base map from a copy of your plat, (or property survey) that most homeowners receive when they purchase their house. A plat typically shows several individual properties and may or may not show structures, including houses. If you don't have a plat, request one from your tax assessor's office; copies are usually available at no cost or for a nominal fee.

In addition to showing property lines, a footprint of the house, and any other significant structures, the plat should show easements and the location of overhead and underground utility lines owned by the county or city. It should also have a legend indicating its drawing scale, which is typically 1:20, meaning that every inch on the paper is equivalent to 20 feet on your property. If the scale isn't shown, you can calculate it by measuring a distance on the plat in inches, and then correlating that with the actual distance on your property.

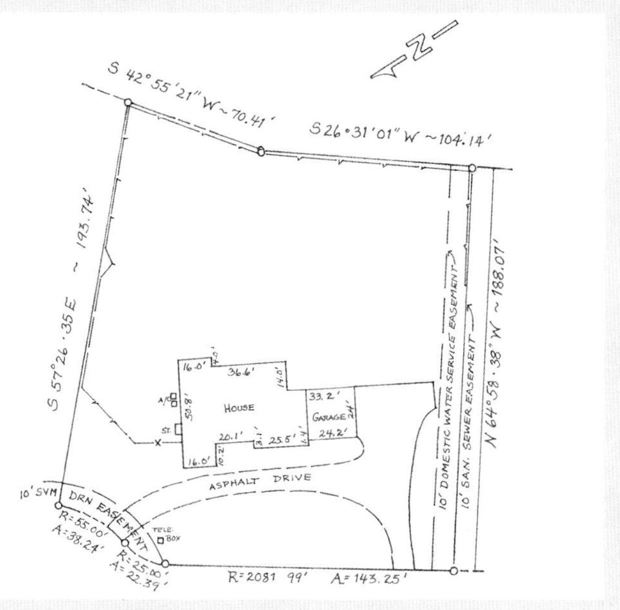

TYPICAL PLAT MAP
A plat map shows the precise boundaries, the measurements of the lot, and the position of the house, garage, and existing easements. Plat maps are available free or for a nominal charge from the tax assessor's office. Make sure you understand where the property lines are and whether any easements exist before you start landscaping.

Make Several Enlarged Copies

Plats are usually a standard size, which is tiny considering all the information you'll want to record. Take your plat or property survey to a copy shop or blueprint company to get an enlargement. While you're there, you might as well make four or five copies, one for your site analysis, one for drawing your design, and extras for updates and changes over the years. If you can, have the blueprint company enlarge the original scale to at least 1:12. This will allow more room to draw garden features.

Even if your map shows the primary dimensions of your property, you'll need to take other measurements. This task will be easier if you use a fiberglass, nylon-clad steel, or chrome-steel measuring tape on a reel. These tapes come in longer lengths than the retractable type and are more suited to measuring larger spaces.

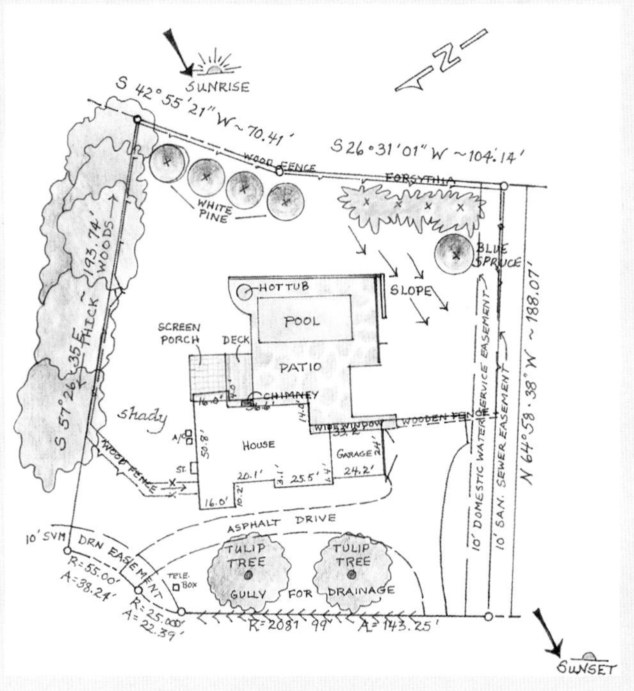

analyze your site

- **Lot boundaries and shape:** Measure other distances as well, such as length of front walk or size of existing patio.
- **Footprint of your home's ground floor:** Note the location of doors leading outside, windows, chimneys, stoops, overhangs, eaves.
- **Structures and paving:** Draw the location of gazebos, fences, walls, and hedges, as well as play structures, patios, decks, terraces, and ponds.
- **Sun and shade patterns:** Map the light and shade patterns throughout the day and year.
- **Utilities and easements:** Note the location of underground electrical cables, water pipes, and sewer pipes or septic systems.
- **Topography and drainage:** Use angled arrows to indicate slopes and changes in elevation. Note areas of water runoff and collection.
- **Microclimates and prevailing winds:** Record warm spots, such as a south-facing wall, or cold pockets in low-lying areas; also note prevailing winds.
- **Existing plantings:** Note the location of beds, trees, and shrubs. Indicate plants with circles scaled to their approximate circumference.
- **Lights and sprinklers:** Mark the location of outdoor lighting fixtures, and, if possible, where the wiring is buried; also note location of in-ground sprinkler heads and pipes.
- **Views, noise sources:** Indicate attractive views you want to highlight and unattractive features, such as street noise, that you wish to de-emphasize.

TOP LEFT On your site map, mark the location of slopes with angled arrows, indicating any features, such as the stairs and bench. If you know the names of the plants in the garden, it's helpful to add that to your data.

TOP RIGHT Make note of views you have of your garden from inside the house. Then, when you are creating your garden design, you can add a vista or garden room that is enjoyable to view from inside the house, as well as when you're outdoors. A path set on an axis seen from the window is alluring, as is a focal point, such as the fountain and arch in the wall, centered on the window.

sun and shade patterns

The interplay of sun and shade changes over the course of the year. When the sun is low in the sky in winter, the shadows cast by the deciduous trees and shrubs are longer than those cast in the summer sun.

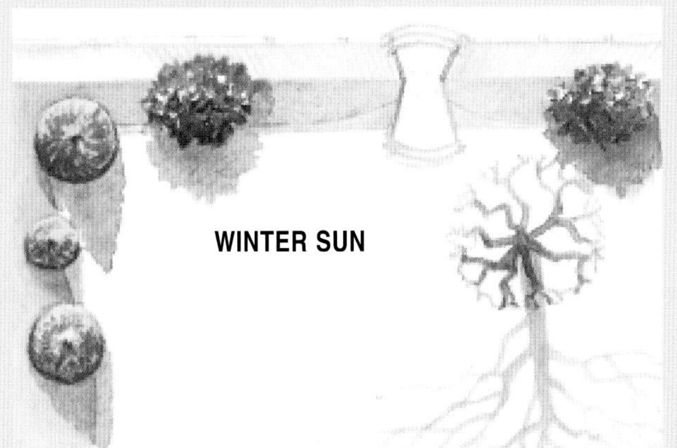

does the light suit your plants?

When you plan your landscape, consider the availability and intensity of light throughout the year. Most plants tolerate a range of light but have specific conditions in which they perform at their best. To determine optimal light conditions for trees, shrubs, and plants, look up the plants or ask your supplier. The following definitions will help you determine which conditions you have on your property.

- **Full Sun**—a daily minimum of six hours of direct, unobstructed sunlight
- **Semi-sunny or partial shade**—a daily minimum of four to six hours of direct sun
- **Light shade or dappled shade**—sunlight under tall trees and under trees with sparse foliage
- **Shade or full shade**—no direct sun; this occurs on the north side of structures and under dense leaf canopies.
- **Dense shade**—shade so deep that no shadows are cast; this occurs between tall buildings and in woods with a dense canopy.

Sun/Shade Log Date

Property Section

Hour	Full Sun	Partial Sun	Full Shade
6:00 am			
8:00 am			
10:00 am			
12:00 noon			
2:00 pm			
4:00 pm			
6:00 pm			
8:00 pm			

To create a sun/shade log for various parts of your property, make photocopies of this chart. Then, monthly during the growing season, check off the hours of full sun.

Equipped with an understanding of design principles and elements, plus a good site analysis, you are ready to begin creating your design. Your property offers you the opportunity to express yourself as though you were a landscape painter, inventing something beautiful from a blank canvas. Instead of paint, your media will be plants, stone, and perhaps brick, sculpture, and garden furniture.

Whether you wish to landscape your property all at once or plant one section at a time as budget and schedule allow, it is a good idea to forge a master plan. Over time you may amend this plan, but it will continue to serve as your basic road map and keep you on course.

Look at your landscape with a fresh eye. For example, instead of leaving the front of the house exposed to the street with just a lawn as a buffer, consider creating a private garden room that serves as a "foyer" to your home. You can do this by planting shrubs around the edge of your property instead of crushing them up against the house foundation. This border could be a hedge such as yew, or a mixture of shrubs and small trees planted to create either an informal hedgerow or a tapestry-like hedge of different foliage colors and textures.

devising your scheme

TOP LEFT A secluded garden spot where you can sit quietly with a good book and a cup of tea can be magical.

CENTER LEFT The ogee arch in the gazebo beautifully frames the view across the water to the house. Foreground plants give depth to the scene.

BOTTOM LEFT Ornamental grasses soften the edges of this pond, lending a naturalistic look to the otherwise structured design. The flagstone patio is a comfortable outdoor room, extending the usable living space of the house during the warm months of the year.

RIGHT A raised pond and fountain is the centerpiece of this patio garden. The retaining walls in the background are made of the same stone as the fountain, providing unity to the design.

BOTTOM RIGHT A naturalistic waterfall is a delightful way to transform a difficult slope into a remarkable garden feature.

your wish list

Before you begin designing, schedule a brainstorming session with your family to come up with a list of features everyone would want in their ideal garden. Allow family members the freedom to think of any idea, no matter how farfetched or expensive. Later, you can determine which suggestions are the most feasible. Your wish list might include:

- Attractive view of the garden from the house
- Places to entertain or dine outside
- Play areas for children
- Private place to retreat
- A water feature
- Space for a plant collection
- A work/storage space screened from view

preparing a budget

Dream landscapes, even fairly simple ones, do not come cheap. Nevertheless, with careful planning and a willingness to do some of the work yourself, you can cut costs.

It is not necessary to implement a landscape plan all at once. In fact, there are advantages to developing the landscape over time. As you live with your garden, you may decide to make modifications to the original plan. To spread out the costs, complete the work in stages. Start with the basic structure of the garden, putting in the hardscape. Follow immediately with slow-growing trees and hedges. Then add to your plan when you have the time and money. Remember, heavy equipment can tear up plantings and compact the ground; finish major hardscaping projects before the plants are in place.

cutting costs

- **Start with small plants.** One-gallon plants cost much less than larger sizes, and small plants tend to adapt to transplanting faster than larger ones.
- **Grow your own.** Sow seeds, propagate plants from cuttings, or divide plants such as daylilies and hostas.
- **Opt for paving instead of grass.** While it is more expensive to install, paving is cheaper to maintain than lawn.
- **Consider gravel or bark paths** rather than brick, stone, or concrete.

should you hire a professional?

Some people have a natural design sense. For those who need help, there are several professional options.

- **Landscape architects** are more expensive than designers because architects have more extensive formal training. To be certified, a landscape architect must have graduated from a course in landscape architecture that includes education in engineering, horticulture, and architectural design. Many states require validating this course work by passing the Landscape Architect Registration Examination (LARE), which tests the candidate's knowledge of grading and drainage, landscape construction, landscape design and history, and professional ethics.
- **Landscape designers** are knowledgeable about design principles and plant materials, especially those frequently used where they live and work. They are not required to have any formal training. These designers are often employed by large nurseries that provide free design services if you purchase plants from them.
- **Landscape contractors** are individuals trained to lay patios and paths, build decks and structures, set up irrigation systems, and install plants. Landscape contractors also carry out the construction plans of landscape architects.

OPPOSITE TOP Free wood chips, delivered by a tree-trimming company, were a bonus for this homeowner's landscape budget. A local tree-trimming company was delighted to save the time and cost of a trip to the city dump.

OPPOSITE BOTTOM Plants with many growing crowns, such as liatris, are good candidates for dividing. Instead of one plant, you can get several, and the smaller plants will grow to full size in a season or two.

BOTTOM LEFT Many plants, including tender geraniums, coleus, impatiens, and roses, root easily from cuttings.

BOTTOM RIGHT Complicated designs that involve engineering may require a landscape architect.

2

Two factors will determine the overall look of your outdoor design: your own taste and what makes sense within the context of your property. You can create a garden that is stylistically pure, adhering completely to the conventions and traditions of a specific style, or you may want to take an eclectic approach, borrowing from different garden motifs to create something completely original. Either way, in this chapter you'll find lots of ideas for introducing international, historic, and regional styles into a unique design that is not only beautiful but well-suited to your landscape and lifestyle.

Garden Styles

- international styles
- three centuries of american design
- american regional traditions

A garden inspired by the Arts and Crafts movement features native plantings and rustic materials that harmonize with the natural surroundings.

international styles

Most countries in the world have developed a distinct, recognizable garden style that reflects their climate, topography, and culture, as well as their emotional, spiritual, and political values. For example, the French are renowned for their elegant, precisely geometric garden designs. A Japanese garden generally conjures images of stone lanterns, meticulously pruned conifers, and zigzag bridges. Think about a Spanish or Mediterranean garden, and you're likely to picture an enclosed courtyard, terracotta paving, brightly painted tiles, and fragrant plants, such as citrus and jasmine.

While each nation does have a typical garden style, it is not unusual for the people of one country to borrow a successful garden-design concept from another nation and make it part of their own tradition. For example, you may think of the *parterre* as a style of flower garden that is French, but it originated in Italy. Chinese gardens, which were first created in monasteries as places for meditation and contemplation, greatly influenced Japanese garden design.

In America, it is no different. The melting pot of cultures and nationalities has brought many foreign garden styles to this country. In some cases, they carefully re-create a look in its pure form. At other times, a design idea from abroad can be adapted to fit particular American needs.

global influences

CLOCKWISE FROM TOP LEFT Examples of international garden styles include Chinese, English, Persian, Japanese, Spanish, Italian, and French.

RIGHT According to the Chinese saying, "Once we have a *ting* (pavilion), we can say we have a garden."

BELOW Chinese zigzag bridges are designed to foil the flow of *sha* (negative energy), which is believed to fly in straight lines.

BOTTOM Water-worn limestone "sculptures" carved by the elements are important features in Chinese gardens.

the Chinese garden: a balance of yin and yang

the English garden: four centuries of elegance

The English have mastered several distinct garden styles. In the eighteenth century, the fashion was for naturalistic landscapes designed to replicate the "perfection" of nature. The Victorian period saw a return to formality. In response to the wealth of new plants discovered around the world, gardeners planted theme gardens displaying a particular plant family, such as ferns or rhododendrons. To show off the new and exotic annuals imported from the tropics, the Victorians mass-planted them using a design technique called "bedding out" or "carpet bedding." (See the photo, left.) In the early twentieth century, garden designers such as William Robinson, Gertrude Jekyll, and Sir Edwin Lutyens pioneered the perennial border and the concept of wild gardens filled with native plants.

OPPOSITE A romantic rose garden, enclosed with a trellis-work fence, is typically English.

OPPOSITE BOTTOM Annuals are massed to create a Persian carpet pattern.

RIGHT Dry stone walls, with plants rooted in the joints and cascading down the face, are typical of the English countryside.

BELOW Towering purple allium globes and foxtail lilies add vertical interest, while boxwood balls and statues temper the exuberance of this late-spring perennial border.

LEFT A sea of grass surrounded by densely planted flowers is very English.

BOTTOM LEFT A cottage garden is a charming jumble of plants.

BOTTOM CENTER Structure combined with informality is the hallmark of an English garden.

BOTTOM RIGHT Honeysuckle scrambles up a brick column.

OPPOSITE Rock gardens are an ideal way to display a collection of small plants.

Victorian gardens: a charming jumble of flowers

bright idea

bold color

Plant in drifts for more impact and a natural look.

the French aesthetic: formal and ornamental

ABOVE *Parterres de broderie* (translated as "embroidered on the ground") are elaborate patterns made from clipped shrubs such as boxwood.

BOTTOM LEFT Avenues—or *allées*—of trees form the framework of French garden style. Scale the concept to your property with appropriately sized trees.

BOTTOM RIGHT In a French *potager*, vegetables, fruits, flowers, and herbs are intermingled to create ornamental patterns. The *parterres* provide structure and frame the composition.

Persian gardens: soothing body and soul

TOP LEFT This walled Western garden introduces Persian features, such as the axial rill leading to the spouting water.

TOP RIGHT The elevated central water feature emphasizes water's life-sustaining properties.

ABOVE Niches for plants and seating give the perception of greater width in this narrow, Persian-style garden.

typical features

Standard features of a Persian garden include walls (the word "paradise" comes from the Persian word for an enclosed garden), water, plants, and Islamic arabesque decorations. The gardens tend to be rectangular, with an axial focal point and a simplicity and clarity of design.

Water is a key element, symbolic of life as well as a refreshing contrast to the arid desert environment of the Middle East. Because water is such a scarce commodity, it is celebrated, but used economically. For example, water will bubble up or pour from spouts, rather than spray into the air, where it evaporates more quickly.

Trees are also important. Elms, willows, and oaks provide shade in summer, and tall cypress filter the dust and reduce the wind flow. Citrus trees are prized for their fruit as well as their fragrant flowers. In keeping with the teachings of the Qur'an, a Persian garden is a life-sustaining oasis, benefiting humans, birds, and animals.

a view of Italy

TOP Evergreen shrubs pruned in the shape of cones create a dramatic, repeating rhythm. The sculpture of the Florentine Boar, believed by many Italians to bring good luck, is a focal point that evokes images of Italy.

ABOVE LEFT The stone balustrades, arches, and columns bring an Italian flavor to this Virginia lakefront terrace.

ABOVE RIGHT A series of ponds, fountains, and statues in wall niches typify the grandeur of the classical Italian garden. The look can be scaled down to fit a smaller space.

RIGHT A multitiered fountain of pure white stone stands out against the dark green avenue of Arborvitae.

FAR RIGHT An urn-shaped fountain and an arbor with classical columns are inspired by Italian design.

classic tuscan style

Italian garden style originated in hilltop villas during the sixteenth century. Characteristic features include garden rooms terraced down a slope that become less formal as they move further away from the house. These "rooms" are furnished with statuary, pergolas (right), columns, stone balustrades, and urns. Typically, Italian gardens have few flowers. Instead, they focus on the rich variety of evergreen foliage, which is used as a textured tapestry to highlight a few flowering plants, a statue, or an ornament. Often, shrubs are pruned as manicured topiary, or laid out in geometrically patterned beds or parterres. This formal, clipped look was copied by the French in their seventeenth-century gardens.

Japanese garden design

OPPOSITE TOP An ancient *Juniperus sabina*, pruned in bonsai style to show off its twisted form, arches over a stone bridge.

LEFT A *Yukimi-gata* (snow viewing) lantern gets its name because snow will accumulate on its large, stone roof. Convention still requires that they be positioned where a light would be useful, such as at the curve of a path or the edge of a pond.

OPPOSITE BOTTOM The textures of a craggy bridge spanning a dry stone river are more striking than fleeting splashes of floral color.

OPPOSITE BOTTOM RIGHT An uneven stone path focuses attention on the walkway.

the **a**sian **w**ay

There are three important elements in a Japanese landscape design. *Water*, a universal symbol of life, is almost always present. Even a dry garden may suggest water with a pebble stream or sand raked in patterns to represent ripples or waves. *Stones* also play an important role and are often assigned special meaning, such as Guardian Stone or Moon Stone. The way these stones are placed in relation to one another has special significance. *Trees and shrubs*, especially evergreens, are the third important element in a Japanese garden. Shrubs trimmed into low, spherical mounds suggest islands or hills.

vibrant Spanish color

Spanish gardens are lively places, rich in pattern and blooming, fragrant plants. Water is an important element, either flowing from a wall fountain or as the focal point of a courtyard. Brightly painted tiles are used prolifically, decorating fountains, benches, walls, and stair risers. Terra-cotta pavers and adobe or stucco walls are topped with flat or arched roof tiles. Archways with potted plants clustered around the uprights are another common embellishment.

TOP LEFT The Moorish influence is strong in Spain, characterized by arches and narrow, decorative waterways. Here is a modern take on the traditional look.

TOP CENTER Spanish gardens vibrate with color from bold flowering plants and architectural features, such as colored stucco, decorative wall tiles, and red-tiled roofs and wall caps.

TOP RIGHT Brightly painted tiles on the risers of a stairway and in a wall mosaic add a Spanish look to a garden, especially when used with adobe or stucco walls and terra-cotta tiles.

LEFT A raised pond and fountain centered in an enclosed courtyard are typical of Spanish gardens. Here the tile-capped wall forming the pool doubles as seating.

OPPOSITE Spanish gardens often feature religious sculpture, such as this statue of St. Francis of Assisi feeding the birds.

three centuries of American design

The history of American garden design can be roughly divided into three hundred-year periods: the eighteenth, nineteenth, and twentieth centuries, or the Colonial, Victorian, and Arts and Crafts periods.

Colonial

The earliest Colonial gardens were "survival plots," designed to provide food and medicinal plants. These fenced gardens were arranged in quadrants intersected by paths, with a bed edging the perimeter. Annual herbs and vegetables were planted in the squares, while perennial herbs and berry bushes grew in the border inside the fence.

As people prospered, city gardens became more elaborate and formal, with symmetrical patterns created by paths and *parterres*. These gardens were designed to convey the message that the owner was affluent, sophisticated, and tasteful.

Victorian

Victorians loved to show off the newly-discovered plants that were being imported from Mexico and South Africa. The technique they used for mass-planting these exotic annuals in elaborate, brightly colored patterns was called "carpet bedding." Victorian gardeners also enjoyed collecting particular plant species, such as ferns, rhododendrons, or geraniums.

Technological breakthroughs transformed gardening in the nineteenth century. The invention of the lawnmower made lawns affordable for the middle classes. Mass-produced cast-iron garden furniture became the rage, and the switch from leather to rubber garden hoses made watering much easier.

Arts and Crafts

By the end of the nineteenth century, a new wave of gardening pioneers rebelled against the more controlled Victorian style, opting for a natural approach to landscape design. They invented mixed borders that combined small trees, shrubs, and flowers and also revived the quaint cottage garden.

For large estates, gardener and journalist William Robinson advocated more structure near the house, flowing into a wild garden of native plants that would merge with the local landscape. The influence of the Arts and Crafts movement is felt in many suburban gardens to this day.

colonial themes

ABOVE A quadrant garden was a popular Colonial motif for both flowers and vegetables. Here, the rectangular beds have been angled at one corner to accommodate the central diamond.

LEFT A cinnabar-red bench in the Chippendale style is a quick way to establish a Colonial theme.

RIGHT Features such as the straw bee skeps (bee shelters, kept under cover to protect them from weather) and the woven wattle fence (made in spring when the twigs and small branches are green and supple), add a Colonial flair to this garden.

ABOVE The posts of this fanciful pergola represent tree trunks, with leafy branches serving as the support brackets.

LEFT To recreate a Victorian garden, select ornate cast iron or aluminum furniture. Aluminum is much lighter than iron, making it easier to move.

victorian touches

A few details that represent the garden style you want to evoke go a long way toward creating the impression you desire. These iron edging hoops, cast to resemble bent twigs, add a Victorian flavor to this garden.

nineteenth-century ornamentation

TOP LEFT A row of fuchsias trained as standards rise above the striped pattern of lobelia, marigolds, wax begonias, Dusty Miller, and petunias.

TOP RIGHT A Victorian-style gazebo goes especially well with a romantic flower garden.

RIGHT The temple-like folly, with its domed, curlicued iron roof, is a lovely focal point in this formal Victorian garden.

RIGHT Architects Charles and Henry Greene combined local stones with clinker bricks that were warped from over firing to make this organic-looking wall for the Gamble House in Pasadena.

ABOVE With it's "cloud lift" motif across the top and fretwork design, this garden gate, designed by Charles Greene in 1911, clearly illustrates the Oriental influence on the work of the Greene brothers.

Charles and Henry Greene

Charles and Henry Greene, brothers who worked in California at the turn of the last century, were one of the most important architectural teams of the Arts and Crafts movement in America. They designed gardens to complement the "ultimate bungalows" they designed for their wealthy clients. To give their gardens a sense of place, they incorporated the local arroyo stones into the garden walls and allowed the garden borders to merge with the local terrain.

TOP LEFT This courtyard garden, designed by Gertrude Jekyll in about 1898, looks as fresh and modern as it did when it was first planted.

TOP RIGHT British gardener William Robinson advocated planting formal gardens near the house and wild gardens, such as this meadow, towards the edge of the property to blend with the surrounding countryside.

RIGHT The herbaceous, or perennial, border was popularized by Gertrude Jekyll, one of the most influential garden writers and designers of the Arts and Crafts movement.

BELOW The Lutyens bench, named after its designer, Edwardian architect Sir Edwin Lutyens (pronounced "Lutchens"), enjoys enduring popularity.

American regional traditions

Just like climate and topography, garden styles differ from one North American region to another. As a rule, gardens tend to reflect local growing conditions as well as the social, historical, and lifestyle variables of the area's first settlers. A traditional Southern garden is as different from a typical California garden as a Japanese garden is from a French one. Gardens with a sense of place, full of plants that are either native to the area or are well adapted to it, will generally feel more harmonious than those that are packed full of every possible exotic. Using local stone or the traditional local building materials for the hardscape also helps root a garden to its locale.

It is important to understand your region's climate and soil conditions: both affect plant hardiness. If you are moving from one part of the country to another, find a good regional garden book to learn what garden designs work best and which plants will thrive.

a sense of place

CLOCKWISE FROM TOP LEFT Midwest, Northeast, South, Pacific Northwest, California, Southwest

LEFT The Oklahoma grassland is evoked in this small suburban garden.

BOTTOM LEFT A prairie garden planted with local natives thrives in downtown Chicago. The feel of the prairie can be captured in a home landscape simply by planting native flowers and grasses in drifts scaled to the size of the lot.

BOTTOM RIGHT The native black-eyed Susan (*Rudbeckia fulgida* 'Goldsturm') stands up to the Midwest climate. Although Chinese in origin, the ornamental grass *Miscanthus sinensis* 'Gracillimus' also adapts well to the region. The grasses add bulk and structure to the design.

the Midwest: a climate of extremes

LEFT Swamp pinks, primroses, and wild sweet William grace the banks of this garden stream.

BOTTOM LEFT The rustic fence made from birch logs roots this Maine garden to its locale.

BOTTOM CENTER Plumbago (*Ceratopteris plumbaginoides*) grows out of the dry stone wall.

BOTTOM RIGHT Instead of cutting down the forest, this homeowner placed his swimming pool in a clearing in the woods.

the Northeast: blending local materials

the South: a graceful symmetry

TOP LEFT Wrought iron is a traditional material for fences and railings in Southern gardens.

TOP RIGHT By dividing this long, narrow town garden into two spaces, each area has better proportions. The design has a formal symmetry in keeping with Charleston, SC, tradition.

LEFT A statue of David is the focal point of this traditional, formal garden with a biblical theme.

ABOVE Walls with gaps between the bricks are decorative as well as practical: they allow cooling breezes to flow through the garden. In Southern gardens, good air circulation is essential during the muggy summer months.

The Southwest is a wide-open region with sweeping desert landscapes accented by ancient mountain ranges that rise up out of the flatlands. The air is hot and dry, and in some places the ground consists of *caliche*, a hard crust of soil that is impenetrable. Southwest garden style reflects the influence of two cultures: the native Indians and the early Spanish settlers, as well as the rigors of the hot, dry climate and stony, alkaline soil. This is an ideal region for growing cacti and other drought-tolerant, heat-loving plants. Residents also create ground covers of stone or gravel.

the Southwest

OPPOSITE This tiered fountain has a cooling effect and is a dramatic focal point in this courtyard patio. Heat-loving sweet alyssum and wax begonias rim the pool.

ABOVE The tree arching over the patio and the arbor that runs along the house provide welcome shade.

TOP RIGHT This tiny swath of lawn is like a jewel set between the drought-resistant ground-cover areas, providing a restful spot with minimal watering requirements.

RIGHT The architecture of this home, inspired by the Pueblo Indians, provides a perfect backdrop to this desert garden of yucca and cacti.

ABOVE A carpet of lawn adds visual excitement to this small garden, creating an illusion of more space than is really there.

BELOW The narrow "rainfall" waterfall pushed against the lot boundary masks any noise from the neighbors and takes up a minimal amount of space.

west coast mix

Blessed with a temperate Mediterranean climate along its coastline, California's gardens reflect its outdoor lifestyle and limited planting space. Because of the state's early history, the Spanish influence is strong. The rainy season lasts about three months in winter, and in some areas, annual rainfall is measured in single digits. As a result, water is celebrated with fountains, ponds, swimming pools, and spas. Drought-tolerant plantings are common, and some new residential developments require owners to plant only California natives.

California style

ABOVE A glass enclosure provides protection from sea breezes without obscuring the spectacular view.

TOP RIGHT Drought-tolerant succulents and cacti provide color and texture in this garden.

RIGHT By cutting into the slope and building a retaining wall, the owners carved out more level land for their patio. Impatiens, which flower year-round, cover the hillside, along with agapanthus, ferns, palms, and shrubs.

the Pacific Northwest

ABOVE Looking upstream from a small bridge provides a front-row view of the lush profusion of azaleas and rhododendrons.

LEFT Lupine and other flowers that can't survive extreme heat thrive in the Pacific Northwest.

BELOW In a mountain garden, a narrow path winds through a naturalized wildflower meadow. Tall conifers ease the transition from open meadow to the forest beyond.

bright idea

add mystery

A partial glimpse of a garden space is tantalizing as well as welcoming.

Asian and English influences

ABOVE English and Asian influences happily combine in this rose-covered moon gate set in a trellis fence. The moon opening is mirrored in the opposite gate.

LEFT *Laburnum*, or golden chain tree, does particularly well in the cool, moist climate of the Pacific Northwest. The yellow flowers play nicely against the blue wisteria and purple *Allium aflatunense*, and the other blue flowers in the border.

3

You can significantly increase the effective living space of your home by creating outdoor garden "rooms." You may want a play space for the children, a cozy spot for alfresco dining, or a secret hideaway where you can get away from it all. Even a small garden can feel bigger when it is divided into more useful areas. With a little thought and effort, your garden can be a warm, welcoming place to spend time with your family, relax with a cup of tea and a book, throw an impromptu cocktail party, or host an elegant soiree.

Outdoor Living Space

- defining your space
- clever garden rooms
- family-friendly play areas
- outdoor dining
- secret retreats
- front gardens

When planned well, even a small backyard space can serve multiple purposes, from coffee and conversation to an intimate dinner party, to a quiet place to read and reflect.

The walls of a garden room can take many forms, including hedges, fences, walls, and trellises. Another way to delineate space is with a change in level. By stepping up or down to reach it, you will feel you've entered a new and distinct room, even without walls or other barriers. As you move from one space to another, a change in paving material or a switch from hardscape to planted ground cover gives the visual impression of a separate garden room. Run a path or perennial border along the edge of the area, and it will act as a boundary defining the room's perimeter. As you think about creating different rooms within your garden, think of the ways you can make each area feel separate yet still part of the whole.

defining your space

ABOVE This small city garden feels larger than it really is because its multilevel design divides the space into two rooms.

RIGHT Three distinct spaces in this small garden are carved out by a combination of grass, pavers, and steps.

OPPOSITE The yew hedges flanking the entrance to this garden room are like the wings on a stage, giving depth to the setting and a sense of mystery about what is on the other side. With its arched niche, the rear hedge helps draw the eye to the "room" beyond.

clever ways to create garden rooms

OPPOSITE The "ante room" to the larger garden space beyond is bounded by shrubs and a small storage shed in the corner with an ogee arch. A corner structure increases the sense of space.

ABOVE A tall hedge encloses this garden room. The visually restful circle of lawn contrasts with the brick's busy basket-weave pattern and the various textures and colors of the shrubs and flowers on either side of the path.

TOP RIGHT Although not physically enclosed, this herb garden feels separate because of the gravel paving encircled by plants.

RIGHT A ring of hornbeam trees creates the walls of this living gazebo.

a room of one's own

TOP LEFT A swirl of brick pavers forms a circle under the hammock, inviting relaxation.

ABOVE LEFT Dividing this long, narrow garden improves its proportions. In the foreground is an oval lawn with space for children to play, while the private space behind serves as a retreat or utility area.

ABOVE RIGHT Crumbling stone walls, statue niches, and the tall "window" at the rear of this garden all suggest a medieval chapel. In the foreground, aromatic herbs grow in the paving spaces.

RIGHT A narrow, pebble-mulched bed and white columns provide a sense of enclosure without making the small space feel claustrophobic. The Spanish-tiled spa doubles as a reflecting pond.

RIGHT Stuccoed to look like adobe and trimmed with antique tiles, this patio fireplace is a wonderful place to congregate with family and friends. It provides warmth on a chilly summer evening.

BELOW A fire pit extends the outdoor season into the spring and autumn months.

bright idea

gas logs

It's easy to light a fire if you plumb for gas instead of burning real wood.

spaces for sharing

ABOVE A window box transforms this prefab garden shed into a charming playhouse. Scaled-down furniture inside a miniature picket fence make this a child-friendly delight.

LEFT A fanciful playhouse woven of green twigs looks as if it has always belonged in this woodland setting.

BELOW Old-fashioned swings hung from a sturdy, vine-covered frame are tempting for both the young and young at heart.

bright idea

ample space

Be generous when you size your deck, especially if that's your primary outdoor space.

family-friendly play areas

ABOVE With its view of surrounding treetops, this deck feels more like a tree house, sure to delight every member of the family.

LEFT The water slide and grotto is made of fiberglass and concrete shaped to look like natural stone. This feature is not only attractive but provides hours of poolside fun.

dining alfresco

OPPOSITE TOP A pretty tablecloth can dress up even the most ordinary table. Add coordinating china and a bowl of bright flowers from the garden, and you have the setting for a memorable meal.

OPPOSITE BOTTOM LEFT Like a semitransparent wall, the trellis provides privacy for this rooftop dining space. Plants cascading from hanging baskets add interest at eye level, and the generously planted containers and raised beds bring color and softness to the hardscape.

OPPOSITE BOTTOM RIGHT A large shade tree combined with wisteria growing on the wall transform this small city patio into a leafy bower.

LEFT An essential feature of an outdoor kitchen is a grill with adjacent countertop space for preparing food. A refrigerator and sink are added conveniences that may increase the value of your home by helping your outdoor kitchen qualify as a second kitchen. The counter opposite the grill defines the space and screens the cooking area from guests.

planning an outdoor kitchen

- Position cooking appliances so that smoke blows away from the seating area.
- For convenience, locate the outdoor kitchen near the house but not where it will be visible *from* the house.
- Arrange the kitchen around the grill. Provide hooks for tongs, spatulas, and other grilling utensils.
- Allow for ample counter space on either side of the grill and on both sides of the sink.
- If space allows, place a counter opposite the grill. It is efficient and keeps children out of the work area.
- For dining counters, provide at least 24 in. of counter width for each stool and 15 in. of leg room underneath.
- In colder areas, disconnect the refrigerator and store it inside during the winter.
- Stainless-steel sinks are preferable outdoors because they won't corrode. In cold climates, install a shutoff valve inside the house to drain the line for winter.
- Include electrical outlets in the cooking and dining areas. Remember, outdoor outlets require ground-fault circuit interrupters (GFCIs).
- Make sure cabinets are weathertight.

LEFT The master bedroom opens onto this private spa garden built along one side of the house.

BOTTOM LEFT A bamboo floor and fence enhance the relaxed, tropical feel of this shady nook, screened from view by trees and shrubs.

BELOW A patio built in a niche created by the house looks out into the garden.

far from the madding crowd

secret **r**etreats

Imagine a secret garden room where you can escape with a cup of tea and a good book. The ideal spot for this private space could be the corner of an asymmetrical lot, the narrow strip at the side of the house, or the far end of the garden. You might even encircle an open area with a hedge or trellis for privacy. Use your imagination to transform your secret retreat into a special place you'll want to visit often. Furnish it with a comfortable chair and, if budget allows, a small fountain, so you can enjoy the soothing burble of falling water.

ABOVE The flagstone paving set in gravel serves as an area rug, providing a smooth, level surface for the furniture.

RIGHT Walking across the vine-covered suspension bridge to the tree house is part of the adventure. This much-loved room does double duty as a private retreat and a party space.

ABOVE The brick path to the front door follows an indirect route, allowing visitors to stroll through the garden along the way.

LEFT The path to this suburban home's entrance consists of huge stone slabs that create the impression of being in the mountains.

front gardens

The path to your front door is your first opportunity to add curb appeal and value to your home. Create an enticing entryway that makes visitors feel welcome. Ideally, you want your front-garden design to reflect the style of your home and have some connection with the rest of the neighborhood. It should provide an engaging experience for people arriving from the street or driveway to your front door. For safety, the walkway should be evenly paved, wide enough to be comfortable, and well-lit at night to enhance the inviting feeling.

ways to welcome guests

ABOVE Inspired by the gardens of Provence, stone stairs curve up to the front door. Clusters of perennials and shrubs cover the slope.

TOP RIGHT Set at a diagonal, the tiled front walkway spills out to the city sidewalk and merges with the driveway.

RIGHT A mix of ground covers (Pachysandra, Liriope, grass) adds texture and pattern to the front garden, illustrating the infinite variety of possible greens.

4

Outdoor lighting can transform the night into a time of enchantment, extending the hours you can spend outdoors and lending drama to your landscape design. The pleasures of lingering at the table after an alfresco summer dinner are enhanced when your surroundings are bathed in a soft glow, punctuated here and there by a spotlighted plant, sculpture, or water feature. On a more practical note, exterior lighting can make nighttime walking more secure, and will also help you to protect your home from intruders.

Let There Be Light

- the well-lit garden
- developing a scheme
- lighting options

Well-placed lighting adds drama to backyard plantings, glints off the pool's dark surface, and highlights the shape and texture of other natural elements.

Outdoor illumination comes in two basic forms: spotlights and floodlights. A spotlight's focused beam strikes a defined area, such as a group of shrubs or the limbs of a tree, creating a distinct line between light and dark. A floodlight's glow is more diffuse, covers a wider expanse, and offers a more subtle transition from bright to shadow.

With an artful combination of these light sources, you can create an interplay of incandescence and mystery that just isn't possible in the daytime.

When you plan your nighttime lighting scheme, use colored lenses and bulbs sparingly. While yellow lights attract fewer insects and can be useful in outdoor seating areas, you don't want their unnatural colors to detract from the beauty of the evening.

the well-lit garden

OPPOSITE The lantern set over the gate is an attractive feature by day and a beautiful source of light by night.

LEFT Seven underwater lights, three in the lowest basin and two each in the next two tiers, shine upward, glowing on the golden stone of the fountain and casting dancing reflections on the underside of the basins.

ABOVE A spotlight directed upward highlights the rough beauty of the peeling bark on this river birch. Another light, set high in a tall tree, shines downward, illuminating the canopy with a moonglow effect.

decorating with light

This flower-like fixture illuminates a section of path at the edge of a bed. The verdigris copper's organic appearance blends with the landscape.

Accent lighting differs from the intense illumination needed for safety and security. Accent lighting, also known as architectural lighting, is primarily decorative. Its main purpose is to create an exciting interplay of light and shadow that lends drama to your garden after dark. Just as you would use special lighting indoors to focus attention on a painting or sculpture, outdoor lighting can play up the artful features of your landscape.

An important component of lighting design is creating contrast. To be effective, light should be complemented by shadow. Of course, you can floodlight your entire property so that every detail is as clearly visible as it is during the day. However, your night garden will be far more striking if you contrast lit areas with darker places.

You can create maximum impact by combining different types of lighting effects. *Uplighting* casts a pool of light upward, and can illuminate a fairly large section of shrubbery or the upper branches of a tree. *Downlighting*, which directs light downward, is excellent for lighting a path or stairway. *Spotlighting*, which is always done from a distance, focuses a narrow beam of light on a specific object. To make use of the shadows and patterns created by light, try *backlighting*, which projects interesting silhouettes onto a surface. *Moonlighting* casts light down from several positions in a tree.

Change also adds interest to lighting design. With a low voltage system, you can easily rearrange lights throughout the year. Highlight the blooming azaleas in spring, then move the lights to showcase a summer display in another spot.

Avoid going overboard with colored lenses or bulbs. Yellow-colored lights can be useful near a patio or outdoor sitting area because they attract fewer flying insects. However, you'll be more pleased with white lights, which enhance the natural colors of the plants and other features in your garden.

This low-profile flare light accents a special plant. These types of lights can be used to lead the way to a special destination.

Low-profile edge lights emphasize the texture of the pavers and cast ever-changing shadows.

The low-profile well light (left) can be turned 360°, changing its focus from the shrub to the river stones.

This rectangular flood light works best on main walkways, where optimal light is needed for walking and security.

casting a glow

ABOVE Evenly spaced underwater lights shine upward, showing off the texture of the stone wall and illuminating a pair of waterfalls. Additional lights behind the wall glow through the glass "windows," giving nocturnal emphasis to the pattern. The waterfall's turbulent power is enhanced when lit from underneath.

RIGHT Experiment to find the perfect angle for a light. To avoid casting unpleasant shadows on the little boy's face, lighting designer Mark Oxley placed the light a bit further from the subject than he would for a tree or shrub, resulting in a soft glow on the sculpture and the nearby plantings.

LEFT Uplights emphasize the texture and pattern of this stone and stucco pool house.

RIGHT A terrace with a spectacular lake view is down-lit with surface deck lights that create a warm, welcoming ambiance.

OPPOSITE TOP RIGHT Uplights behind the foliage create shadowy patterns on the column.

RIGHT Fairy lights wrapped around tree trunks create a festive air. Paper lanterns strung from the trees look like multiple moons hovering over the garden.

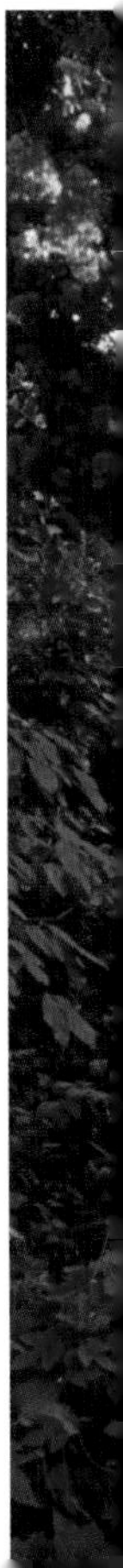

bright idea

overhead lighting

Subtle downlighting casts a glow much like a full moon, shedding soft light through the leaves overhanging this garden path.

moods, patterns, and textures

Before you purchase lights and wires, take time to assess your landscape by day. Think about where you want the perimeter of the nighttime garden to be so you can define the space with a "wall" of lights. Choose one or two striking features you would like to emphasize, such as a specimen plant, sculpture, or arbor. Eyes naturally adjust to seeing in the dark, so be cautious about over-lighting your space. If an area is uniformly bright, you will lose the power and atmosphere of nuanced light. In most gardens, a sense of mystery, with a few plants and features barely suggested by subtle lighting, is far more effective than the brazen atmosphere of Times Square.

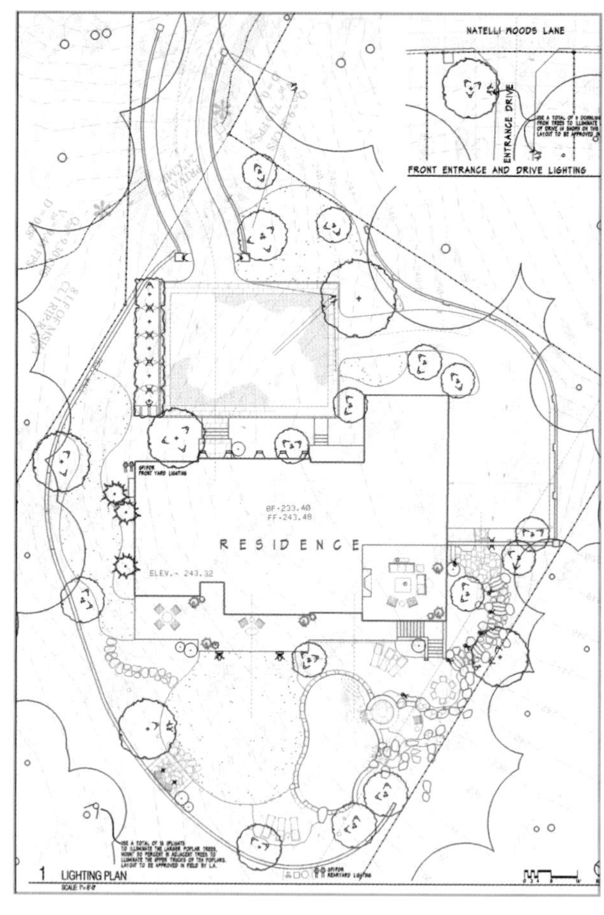

developing a scheme

ABOVE Use a copy of your garden plat or a blueprint of the garden design to map out your lighting plan. For a complex job, especially one involving the placement of lights high in trees, you may consider hiring a professional. One good way to find a good designer is to scout neighborhoods at night to find homes with effective landscape lighting. Approach the owners either by knocking on their door or by sending a letter, and ask for a referral. Most people will be flattered by your interest and happy to share their designer's name.

LEFT A good lighting plan uses a variety of lighting techniques to create a captivating effect.

installing low-voltage lights

The toughest part of installing low-voltage lights is deciding where you want them and what effect you would like to create. This type of lighting is easy to handle and install, and there are many pre-packaged starter kits on the market that are designed to meet specific purposes. Low-voltage lights use transformers to reduce your home's voltage from the standard 110/120 volts to a safer 12 volts. Transformers are plugged into an outside outlet, and the wire is laid in the ground. Lighting fixtures clip onto the wire at any point you select. Once you're ready to connect the wires, the job literally takes minutes. Avoid crossing the wire back over itself or making tight, twisty turns. Be careful not to exceed the prescribed number of lights for each circuit. Plug the transformer box into a properly installed outdoor outlet. If you don't have an outdoor outlet, have one installed by a professional electrician following local codes.

Tools and Materials: lights, fixtures, wires, transformer box, measuring tape to mark the spacing between lights, wire cutters (with a stripper), pliers, screwdriver to assemble the light fixtures and connect wires.

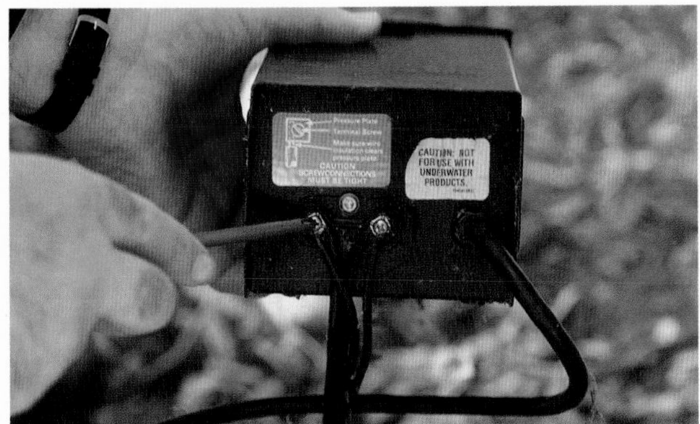

1 **Connect the wire cable to the transformer box.** Wrap the wire around the terminal screws. For proper connection, make sure the wire insulation is clear of the pressure plates. Tighten the screws firmly, and plug the box into a grounded outlet.

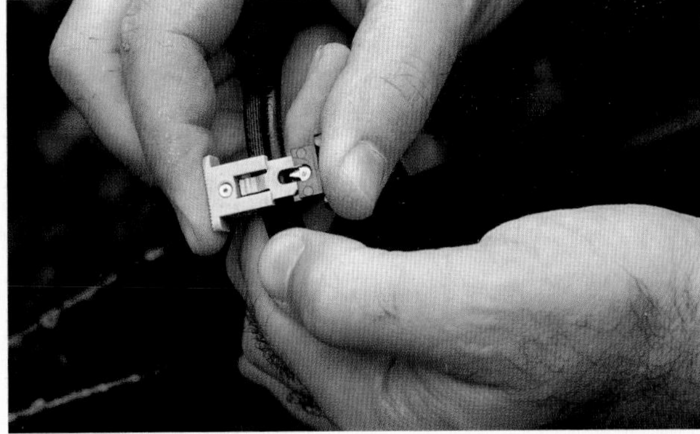

2 **Connect the lamps to the low-voltage cable.** Pinch the fast-lock connector, attached to the cable that runs from the light, onto the main line. You can undo the connection and move it at any time. The hole is tiny and the voltage is low, so there is no chance for a shock.

3 **Hide the wires.** Pre-installed wires run through the light fixture and are connected to the main line. You can bury the cable lines underground. But if you think you may be moving the system, the lines are perfectly safe left aboveground.

4 **Position the lamp.** Anchor the lamp in place by pressing the lamp stake into the ground. In climates where heavy winter freezes cause heaving, dig an 8 x 6-in. hole for the lamp stake, and backfill the hole with gravel.

lighting charts the course of a garden journey

OPPOSITE Lighting helps define the journey through this garden at night. Low lights line the brick path, and spotlights shine upward, focusing on the columns of the arbor. The illuminated fountain in the distance draws the eye, creating a focal point and desired destination.

ABOVE A pair of wall-mounted lanterns shed purposeful light on the patio. When romance is on the menu, just the candelabras are used.

BELOW In addition to the overhead lantern, which sheds light on the table in the arbor, each column is highlighted with a downward-facing spotlight. Fixtures on risers provide circles of light around the pool, and uplit trees in the background define the boundaries of this nocturnal garden space.

light ideas

Transition gradually from a brightly lit area to a dark spot with a soft layer of light in between.

The eye tends to bounce back and forth between two equal areas of light. Instead, use an odd number of lights to create an asymmetrical lighting design, and position them so the eye is led from one lit area to the next.

Create rhythm with garden lights by illuminating items in a row.

Use lights to define the nighttime "walls" of a garden room. A dark area beyond the lights will appear as walls.

Strive for a balance between mass (dark areas) and space (lighted areas). Too much dark is unwelcoming and unsafe; too much light makes the space uninteresting.

Use a downward-facing spotlight above a tree with an open, lacy canopy to create pretty shadow patterns on the ground.

Take advantage of the reflective properties of pale colored flowers and foliage.

fixture options

- **Bollard lights:** Cylindrical fixtures with faceted lenses; diffuse light downward and outward; useful for lighting paths and walkways
- **Floodlights:** Perfect for illuminating a wall or other large object
- **Spotlights:** Good for highlighting focal points such as flowers or statues
- **Globe lights:** Clear or frosted for general diffused illumination
- **Lanterns:** Fixtures that provide ambient light from three or four sides; have the potential to create glare
- **Mushroom lights:** Usually mounted on a riser stalk and topped with a rounded cap; focus downward with no outward spread; useful for lighting borders, walkways, and low foliage
- **Surface deck lights:** Compact, flat fixtures designed for mounting on side of decks, benches, and stair railings for discrete, diffused light without glare
- **Tier lights:** Often with angled shades arranged in tiers to direct light downward and outward; usually mounted on stalks to provide wide pools of light for walkways and steps
- **Well lights:** Spotlights housed in weather-resistant tubes and buried in the ground to hide light source; good for uplighting trees and shrubs

TOP LEFT Topped with a weathervane, this lantern provides illumination from four sides, creating a cheerful, welcoming atmosphere around the area.

ABOVE Mushroom-shaped fixtures point downward, creating pools of light along the brick path.

OPPOSITE TOP Two spotlights focused on the underside of this Japanese black pine bathe it with warm light.

RIGHT This spotlight is directed to uplight the crape myrtle and nearby hosta.

in the market

Inexpensive fixtures may not be a bargain if they wear out quickly and need excessive maintenance to keep them working. Invest in the best quality light fixtures your budget will allow. Here are features to look for when you're ready to shop for your outdoor light fixtures.

- **Waterproof casing.** Lenses should be sealed and gasketed to their housings.
- **Adjustability.** You'll want the option to choose between wider or narrower light beams, as well as different bulb wattages.
- **Versatility.** For maximum versatility, choose fixtures that accept accessories such as shrouds, louvers, lenses, and color filters.
- **Maintenance.** Your fixtures should accept long-life bulbs, and lightbulbs should be easy to change.
- **Corrosion resistance.** Copper and brass are best. Cast iron is prone to corrosion; aluminum and aluminum alloys coated with a corrosion-resistant substance are fine except in coastal zones, in acidic soil, or in hot desert areas.
- **Non-plastic parts.** Avoid fixtures made of plastic or with plastic components; they become brittle when exposed to ultraviolet light.

5

There are all sorts of techniques you can use to turn plants into the star players in your garden. By selecting from the brilliant palette that nature provides, you can form beautiful pictures that either burst with bright colors, or quietly seduce the eye with a single hue. You might choose to spotlight the drama of a tree's intertwined branches; the cunning shape of a hedge sculpted to resemble a swan; or a holly that has been trained on a single stem, topped with foliage reminiscent of an oversized lollipop. Even everyday vegetables can provide a melange of tints and leafy textures.

Planting Designs

- garden compositions
- color-themed gardens
- living walls and partitions
- charming topiaries
- knot gardens
- plants for drama
- vegetable gardens

This purple and black composition is rich with textures provided by an unexpected combination of plants such as cabbages, allium, and New Zealand flax.

create beautiful pictures with plants

ABOVE The orange-flowering rose 'Chris Evert' is underplanted with white campion and the variegated society garlic 'Silver Lace'. Perennials and annuals grown as underplantings in a rose garden help hide the rose's bare legs.

RIGHT A stepping-stone path winds through a variety of herbs including purple *Perilla frutescens*, silvery gray lamb's ears, creeping thyme, and purple basil.

ABOVE LEFT A collection of herbs is displayed in beds divided by narrow brick paths that allow access for harvesting. Sweet alyssum rims the outer edge of the garden.

ABOVE Low boxwood hedges lend structure to this bountiful collection of roses.

LEFT A giant bird of paradise (*Strelitzia nicolai*) makes a dramatic statement in this tropical garden.

garden compositions

"Whether it is the putting together of two or three kinds of plants, or even of one kind only in some happy setting...the intention is always the same—to use the plants to the best of one's means and intelligence so as to form pictures of living beauty." So wrote British garden designer Gertrude Jekyll in her 1908 book, *Color Schemes for the Flower Garden*. A century later, today's gardeners find that her words still ring true. Thanks to an amazing palette of plants and new, improved hybrids introduced every year, it is both fun and challenging to combine plants, often called *softscaping*, with *hardscaping* elements such as rocks, paths, and walls, to create "beautiful pictures" that express your own personal style.

color-themed gardens

OPPOSITE Blue and lavender flowers, such as Jacob's ladder, Allium 'Purple Sensation', pincushion flower, and columbine, are combined with white-flowering woodrush (*Luzula nivea*) to create a vividly colored planting.

LEFT Bold, yellow-striped canna leaves and large yellow daylilies make a bright pairing in this garden.

BELOW This border is planted with yellow-hued trees and shrubs, including false cypress 'Sungold', elder flower 'Sutherland Gold', and honey locust 'Sunburst'.

RIGHT A white-flowering foxglove, hydrangea, Marguerite daisy, and the climbing rose 'Seagull' are combined to form a pristine white garden. Silvery gray and pale yellow add touches of warmth.

moon gardens

A white "moon" garden filled with night-blooming and pale-colored flowers that reflect moonlight is ideal for people who want to enjoy their landscape after dark. Plant your moon garden near the patio so you can gaze at the white blossoms when you dine outdoors.

Many flowers, such as night jessamine, angel's trumpets, gardenia, *Hosta plantaginea*, sweet peas, roses, Phlox 'David', and honeysuckle release their scent at night. Others, such as moonflowers, four-o'clocks, *Datura inoxia*, and some water lilies open in the late afternoon, showing off their floral splendor in the evening hours.

Don't forget to include foliage with splashes or ribbons of white or silver, such as *Cornus alba* 'Elegantissima' (variegated red-stemmed dogwood), and hostas including *H. albomarginata*. These plants will add another pale accent, maintaining interest after the flowers are spent.

LEFT The lower trunks of these hornbeam trees are kept clean and the upper branches pruned to create a hedge on "stilts." This hedge is ideal along a property line for screening the neighbor's house from view without using too much space in the bed underneath.

BOTTOM Two English-lavender hybrids create an undulating wave of color when this hedge is in bloom. Prune lavender hedges after they flower to maintain their shape and renew the plants.

RIGHT Planted along the edge of the woods, this hedge looks most natural when left unpruned.

RIGHT The dark-green yew hedge sets off the silver lamb's ears "mini-hedge" at its feet.

OPPOSITE FAR RIGHT This green hedge provides the perfect neutral background to show off the white roses and gray foliage of the Swiss willow (*Salix helvetica*) that stands in pleasing contrast to the dark-green yew.

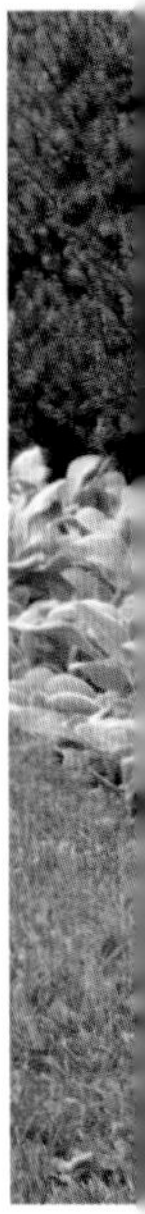

bright idea

mix it up

Create a tapestry effect by planting a hedge of mixed shrubs with different foliage colors and textures.

the charm of topiaries

OPPOSITE TOP LEFT Variegated ivy trained over a wire frame makes an attractive focal point set on a pedestal or tabletop.

ABOVE Pairs of double tetrahedrons flank these stairs, lending weight and importance to the scene.

OPPOSITE BOTTOM At Monkton, Maryland's Ladew Topiary Gardens, leafy swans "swim" atop billowing yew hedges.

TOP RIGHT In this California garden, a sculpture of Mr. McGregor chasing Peter Rabbit is made from creeping fig (*Ficus pumila*) over a sphagnum moss-stuffed wire frame.

RIGHT A variegated holly (*Ilex aquifolium* 'Golden Queen') is trained in a lollipop form.

LEFT Lettuces planted in a repeating diamond pattern form this knot garden, a formal type of garden design that was first established during the reign of Elizabeth I.

BELOW This knot is only about 12 feet in diameter and doesn't require a lot of pruning. Colored stones emphasize the pattern.

RIGHT Green and variegated boxwood combined with germander are pruned to create an intricate pattern of ribbons that appear to weave over and under each other. The central sphere made of false olive (*Phillyrea angustifolia*) requires meticulous pruning to maintain its shape.

precisely pruned knot gardens

outstanding plants for drama

OPPOSITE A venerable cedar of Lebanon tree casts a long shadow, duplicating itself in the pond's reflection.

ABOVE A double row of queen palms has greater impact on this garden composition than a single tree. Parallel rows of eight tall trunks create a repeating rhythm, while the ninth tree takes center stage at the end of the "avenue."

TOP RIGHT With their twisty intertwined branches, Japanese maple trees make great year-round focal points.

RIGHT Ringed by a low boxwood hedge, the twisted juniper is positioned to shine in this garden.

ABOVE Interplanting edible flowers and vegetables in raised beds creates an orderly and attractive display that is easy to tend.

TOP RIGHT A variety of lettuces combine to form this "salad bowl." Most vegetables will grow happily in containers if given enough root room.

RIGHT With easy access to the kitchen, this vegetable garden—featuring lettuces, cabbages, and broccoli—is a visual medley of colors and leafy textures.

OPPOSITE Vegetables don't need to be planted in perfect ranks. This bark path wends its way through freeform beds planted with a bounty of flowers and vegetables, including pumpkins and cabbages.

bountiful vegetable gardens

6

Every garden needs an accent or two to punctuate the landscape design and communicate the personality and taste of its owners. In addition to being attractive focal points, details such as fences, walkways, and gates provide structure, organization, and boundaries to an otherwise relaxed design. Others, such as sculptures, fountains, and waterfalls, are meant to be enjoyed for their soothing beauty alone. In every case, proper design and placement of your garden's accents are the key to achieving a polished setting.

Accent on the Garden

- structural statements
- garden pathways
- special touches
- water features
- in and out of sight
- places to perch

Flanders poppies *(Papaver rhoeas)* grow exuberantly through this bench, making sitting a bit ticklish, but adding romance and charm to this garden setting.

LEFT A vine-covered arbor with a built-in bench creates a sun-dappled retreat in this woodland garden.

BELOW A circular stone patio shaded by a leafy arbor is an attractive focal point and alluring destination in the garden.

OPPOSITE With its rows of columns supporting an open roof, this pergola creates a dramatic passageway between two garden rooms.

structural statements

You can achieve instant shade and add a stunning architectural accent with an arbor or pergola. These vertical structures work particularly well as transitions between different areas of your garden. Grow lush vines around the support posts, and hang baskets filled with shade-loving begonias or cascading fuchsias from the overhead beams.

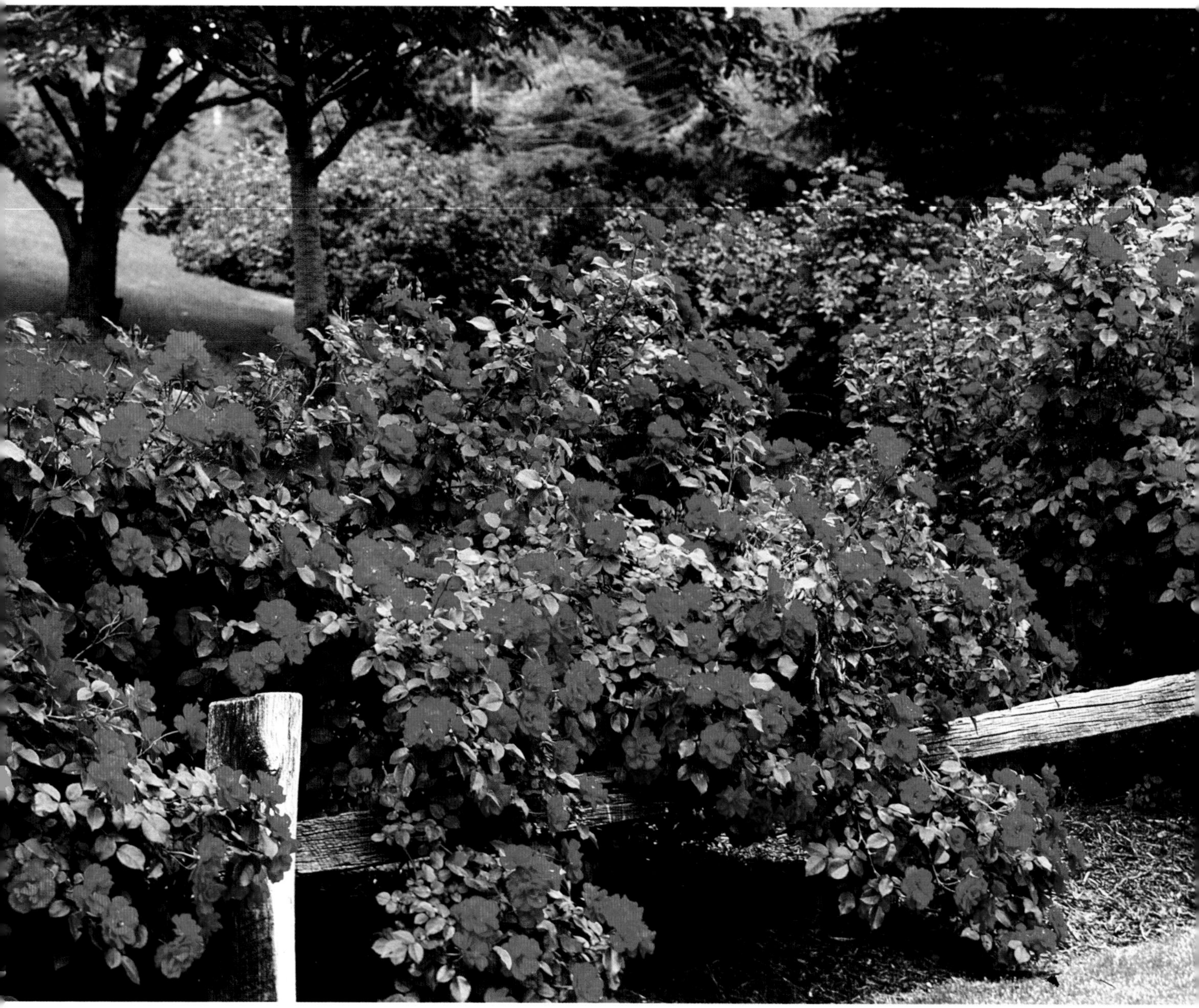

fencing choices for slopes

Slopes present special challenges for fence designs because the sections are generally straight and parallel with the ground. Three possible solutions include a *stepped fence*, which allows gaps to occur as the slope progresses downward; a *sloped fence*, which follows the hillside so that the top of the fence is angled at the same degree as the slope; and a *contoured fence*, which is custom-built so that each paling (picket) touches the ground, creating a wavy line across the top and bottom.

Stepped Fencing

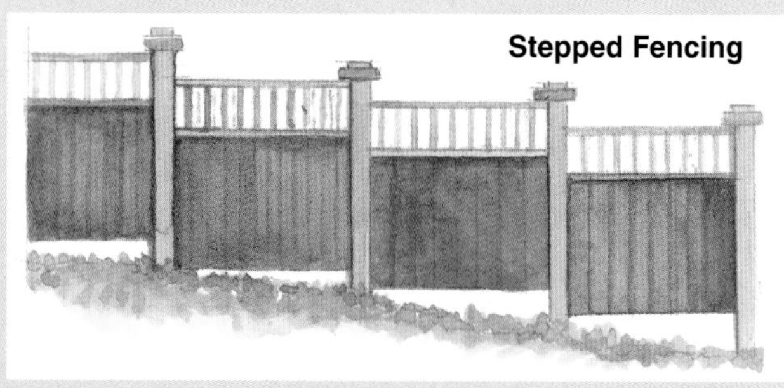

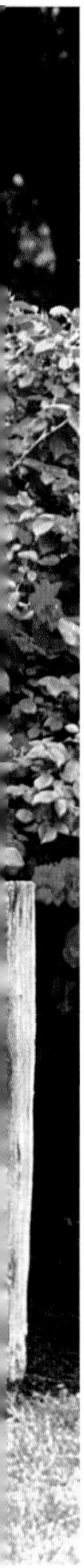

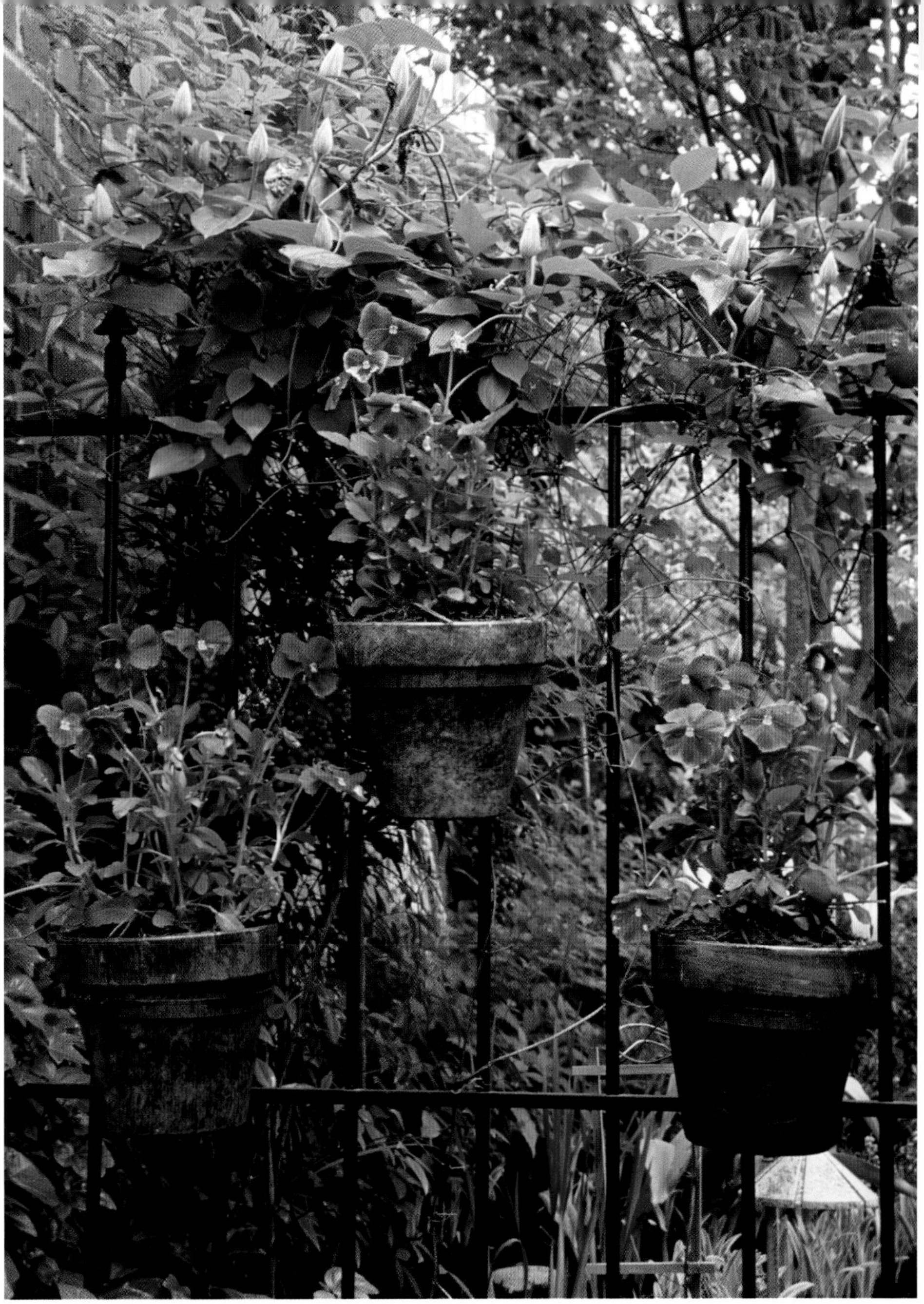

LEFT A rustic split-rail fence looks festive draped with the Meidiland shrub rose 'Sevillana', a pest- and disease-resistant variety that flowers throughout the summer.

RIGHT Flower pots hung from an ironwork fence bring bursts of color to eye level. A budding clematis vine twines through the bars, adding to the cheerful display.

fencing options

Sloped Fencing

Contour Fencing

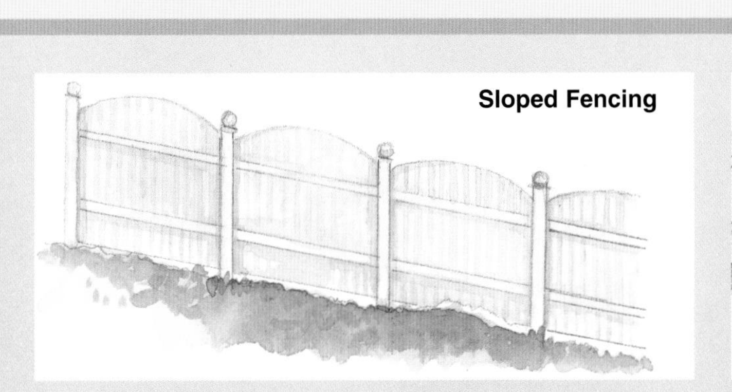

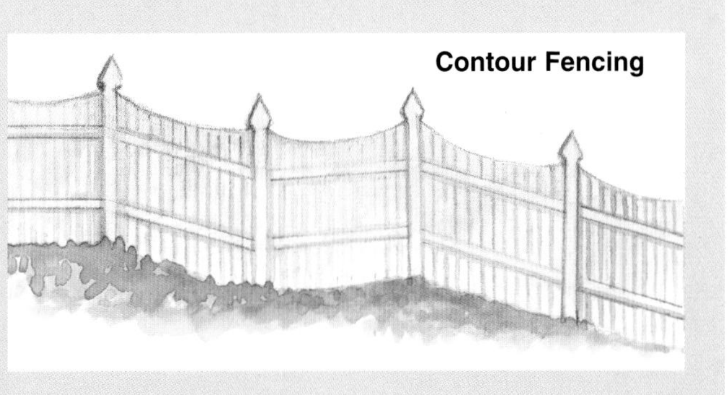

TOP LEFT The grid pattern in the gate is echoed in the walkway and matches the cutout design in the wall.

MIDDLE LEFT The whimsy of this custom-made gate reflects the homeowner's personality.

BOTTOM LEFT A pergola gate topper set into river-stone pillars adds interest to this Craftsman-inspired design.

BELOW The arbor arching over this picket gate sets a romantic mood that is perfect for a cottage garden.

RIGHT Handsome, vintage iron gates are available in many antique stores. You can hang them on hinges set in brick or stone pillars or from iron posts as seen here.

RIGHT This unusual gate features a concentric ring pattern on its sawn log ends.

BOTTOM RIGHT When ajar, the solid wooden gate beckons visitors to enter the garden; when shut, it provides complete privacy.

an open gate beckons you to enter

OPPOSITE TOP LEFT Situated on a grassy slope across from the house, this gazebo provides a focal point in this informal landscape design.

OPPOSITE BOTTOM RIGHT A large Victorian-style gazebo is a destination in this woodland garden. Vents in the roof help keep it cool.

gazebos, temples, and follies

ABOVE Award-winning designer Julie Toll created this living gazebo, formed by training the supple trunks of nine young whitebeam (*Sorbia aria*) trees to form an arched ceiling. The branches are woven together using a technique called pleaching.

RIGHT Built into the dock, this gazebo is just big enough for a hammock, an ideal spot for a lakeside snooze.

what is a folly?

"Folly" is the term given to any garden structure that serves no real purpose except to provide a pleasing focal point. On English estates in the eighteenth and nineteenth centuries, follies often took the form of stone towers or Greek temples (top right), and were built on a hill where they could be seen from a distance. Popular motifs in country-estate gardens included fake ruins and grottoes inspired by trips to Italy. This modern garden folly (bottom right) is a witty interpretation of a Greek Doric design.

bright idea

gazebo screens

Screen in a gazebo to keep out flying pests.

garden pathways

In addition to the practical task of getting people through the garden without muddying their shoes, paths help to choreograph the way you'd like visitors to move through your landscape. For example, a wide, straight path puts the focus on the destination. A narrow path that meanders through the landscape encourages a slower journey, allowing the traveler to pause along the way and smell the flowers. Depending on the size of your garden, you may have one path that serves as a primary artery, connected to smaller walkways that lead to out-of-the-way corners.

OPPOSITE TOP This Chippendale-style bridge is full of delightful mischief. Each bird perched along the top rail spouts arcs of water that flow in an intricate pattern. Although cinnabar is a strong color, it adds zest to most garden settings.

OPPOSITE BOTTOM In a Japanese-style garden, a stone slab bridge spans a dry gravel riverbed, enhancing the illusion of a stream running through the landscape.

RIGHT Wooden planks laid two abreast form this zigzag bridge that brings walkers close to the lush bog foliage. Asian in origin, zigzag bridges are designed to focus the walker's attention on the journey.

paths both rough and refined

OPPOSITE This path's square flagstones are rotated 90 deg., emboldening the walkway that cuts diagonally through this garden.

ABOVE Tile and stone combine to create a diamond pattern on this walkway. The gate and the trellis surrounding the front door echo the motif.

TOP RIGHT A gravel path with an open-weave brick pattern is less expensive to build than a solid-brick path. The edging contains the gravel so it doesn't drift into the beds.

RIGHT A double row of paving squares makes walking more comfortable and enhances the importance of the path.

LEFT The stairs' daisy-filled containers flare out, seeming to embrace visitors.

BELOW The stone stairs merge seamlessly with the lawn, creating an arresting sculptural pattern.

OPPOSITE TOP Drought-tolerant, heat-loving plants, such as sweet alyssum, do well when planted in the risers of garden stairs.

OPPOSITE BOTTOM LEFT Climbing red roses entwined between the iron railings soften the entrance of this house.

OPPOSITE BOTTOM RIGHT Plants blend in with the stairs, blurring the line between garden and path.

step by step on the garden journey

LEFT A small patch of well-manicured lawn in the center of the garden gives the eye a place to rest.

RIGHT Beds act as screens so you don't see the lawn and garden all at once, creating a delightful sense of discovery.

BOTTOM RIGHT A clean-cut edge gives this lawn a tidy, tailored appearance.

bright idea

bulbs in the lawn

Drifts of early flowering bulbs, such as crocus, daffodils, *Muscari* (grape hyacinth), *Ipheion* (starflower), and *Scilla,* planted in the lawn, bring color to a late winter garden. Let the bulb foliage die back before you mow.

ABOVE Where shade is intense, grow moss instead of grass. It requires no mowing or fertilizing, stays green all winter, and tolerates foot traffic.

BELOW By removing the lower branches of the tulip poplar trees, the owners obtained enough sun to grow grass in this wooded garden.

lush lawns invite barefoot strolls

bright idea

pot inside a pot

Place a small pot inside a larger one, fill the space between with potting mix, and plant ivy around the rim. Plant flowers in the inner pot.

special touches

Containers add color and excitement to patios, stairs, and walkways. Find planters that complement your garden style, and match your plants with pots that suit their height and growing habits. Showy plants, such as palms and formally-pruned shrubs, shine in classic urns; cascading, natural arrangements look great in a rustic half barrel or an old farm trough.

container gardening

OPPOSITE BOTTOM A painted farm trough planted with an ornamental rice plant (*Oryza sativa* 'Red Dragon') coordinates with the *Coleus* 'Copper Glow' foliage across the pool.

ABOVE LEFT Orange terra-cotta mulch complements the foliage of the *Cordyline* 'Red Star' planted in this glowing silver container. Other offbeat mulch possibilities include colored glass beads, nutshells, and bits of metal hardware such as nuts and washers.

ABOVE RIGHT Four brush cherry (*Eugenia myrtifolia*) shrubs trained as standards frame the axis of this design. Although they are frost tender, these plants can overwinter indoors.

RIGHT Strawberry pots are great for any shallow-rooted cascading plants, such as these creeping thymes.

LEFT A bougainvillaea is shaped in an informal pattern. Almost any tree or shrub is suitable for espalier if it is trained when it is young.

ABOVE Espaliered fruit trees take up less space in the garden and bear more fruit at a younger age. Here, a dwarf peach tree is trained in a palmate (fan-shaped) form.

OPPOSITE LEFT A young fruit tree is being trained in a U-shaped candelabra form. The warmth from the brick wall will help ripen the fruit earlier in the season.

OPPOSITE RIGHT Fiery pyracantha berries make a dramatic statement against this wall; in spring, small, white flowers will create a different view.

espalier: the fine art of tree shaping

bright idea

outlined shape

Erect your support frame in the early training stages so you can see where you're going.

TOP LEFT Even an inexpensive ornament can add charm and personality to the garden.

MIDDLE LEFT These rabbits are welcome additions to the lettuce bed, and they can be moved elsewhere when the crop is finished.

BOTTOM LEFT The texture and shape of the pineapple, a symbol of hospitality, is echoed in the *Euphorbia characias wulfenii* in the background.

TOP RIGHT A sculpture of a seated woman by Francisco Zuñiga overlooks the garden from her perch in front of an Australian tree fern.

BOTTOM RIGHT Because it was too deeply rooted to remove, the homeowners made this boulder a highlight of their garden, topping the massive rock with delicate statues by Peggy Walton Packard.

sculpture and ornaments

bright idea

turn problems into assets

With imagination, most garden problems can be turned into assets. This mossy boulder (right) became a central focus of the lawn.

keeping **t**hem **s**afe

Sadly, the theft of garden ornaments is on the rise. Protect valuable statuary by keeping them out of sight from the street or by ensuring that they are securely fastened so they cannot be removed. Don't lull yourself into a false sense of security simply because an item is heavy. Thieves have been known to cart away very large items and to cut off bench legs at ground level when they are imbedded in concrete.

sundials and armillary spheres

ABOVE LEFT Positioned as the focal point in the boxwood garden room, this classical sundial is well-suited to its setting.

ABOVE RIGHT The craft of sundial making continues to flourish today. Modern artisans combine sculpting techniques with the mathematical discipline of engineers.

RIGHT Several varieties of creeping thyme planted in the spaces between the hours of this monumental sundial create an inside joke for those who recognize the plant.

OPPOSITE The armillary was first invented in 255 B.C. by the Greek astronomer Eratosthenes as a model of the celestial sphere. The sleek lines of this modern version fit well with the bold foliage in this garden.

setting the right time

In order to keep the correct time, a horizontal sundial must be calibrated to your location.

1. Set the *gnomon* (the sundial arm that casts the shadow) so the upper angled edge, or style, is equal to the latitude of your house. For example, at 33 deg. north latitude, use a protractor to determine the exact angle for 33 deg. Then shim the face of the dial, adjusting it until the style sits at that angle.
2. In the northern hemisphere, the gnomon should point to the number 12, and must also face the North Star, which is geographic or true north. To determine geographic north, level the surface where you plan to set the dial.
3. Draw several concentric circles on the ground centered on the spot for the sundial. One circle will do, but if you make several, you are not tied to a specific time of day to take your measurements.
4. Fix a dowel or stake into the ground at the exact center of the circles, making sure the stick is absolutely perpendicular to the ground.
5. In the morning, watch the shadow cast by the dowel, and mark the point where it touches one of the circles.
6. Go back in the afternoon and watch for the shadow to touch the same circle on the opposite side. If you make the first mark at 9 in the morning, you can expect the shadow to hit the circle on the opposite side at about 3 P.M., six hours later. Mark that point and draw a line between two. Draw another line that bisects the first at right angles. Position the sundial so the gnomon points north along the second line.

water features

Throughout the ages, gardeners have used pools, ponds, and fountains to enliven their landscapes and refresh their spirits. Wide, still pools produce magical reflections in their mirror-like surfaces; while fountains and waterfalls create sounds ranging from a soothing splash to a lively chatter. Even an urban patio has room for a small fountain mounted on a wall. The choice depends on what fits best in your design plan.

OPPOSITE TOP An oversize terra-cotta teapot and cup are a charming fountain feature.

OPPOSITE BOTTOM Lively jets of water are trained to arc over the pool.

ABOVE The acrylic-and-stainless-steel AquaSphere fountain designed by Allison Armour-Wilson mixes classic forms with modern materials.

RIGHT Water spills from five tiered fountains before running into a narrow rill that traverses this small deck.

BOTTOM RIGHT The family Weimaraner was the model for this whimsical fountain.

bright idea

recess fountain heads

Prevent stubbed toes by recessing fountain heads that are set in the pavement.

ABOVE Primrose and other moisture-loving plants encircle this garden pond. By growing a variety of primrose species, you can have blooms from late winter through the middle of summer.

facts on flexible pond liners

When the pond you plan does not conform to a preformed rigid liner, you can opt for a flexible liner. Flexible pond liners are available in your choice of three different materials:

- **Polyethylene** should only be used for temporary ponds. This material tears easily and cracks after extended exposure to sunlight. If you install a double layer of 500-gauge sheeting, most brands will last at least two to three years.
- **Polyvinyl chloride (PVC)** is the mid-priced option. Strong and stretchable, PVC has a life span of 10 to 15 years, making it much more durable than polyethylene, but not as long-lasting as synthetic rubber. An upgraded version, PVC-E, is guaranteed for 10 years.
- **Synthetic rubber sheeting** is the latest breakthrough in pond technology. Two types on the market are ethylene propylene diene monomer (EPDM) and butyl rubber. Both are durable, flexible materials that are safe for all aquatic life. Synthetic rubber is impervious to sunlight, frost, and air pollution, and its elasticity allows the liner to "give" when subjected to ice pressure and earth movement. This stretchable quality makes it better than cement-lined ponds, which tend to crack under stress. Although synthetic rubber sheeting is considerably more expensive than PVC, it is a reasonable investment if you want your pond to endure for decades.

TOP RIGHT The tile pattern in this shallow pond is echoed in the boxwood *parterre* design.

MIDDLE RIGHT Tucked up against the garden wall, this long reflecting pool leaves plenty of patio space for outdoor seating. Pairs of potted cypress add a feathery vertical element to the design.

BOTTOM RIGHT A submersible mist fogger has an ultrasonic pump that vibrates to create a cooling vapor.

BELOW Stones rimming this pond hide the liner and add a rough, natural finish to the edge.

TOP LEFT The swim spa is a combination of whirlpool and swimming pool. In addition to whirlpool jets, a large jet at one end produces a current strong enough to swim against. This hybrid pool is ideal for tiny lots where a full-sized pool won't fit.

swimming pools

MIDDLE LEFT The paint for the bottom of the pool was custom mixed to resemble the deep blue of a lagoon. Blue scaevola, which flowers all summer, contrasts beautifully with the water.

BOTTOM LEFT Water tumbles from the spa over a jumble of local arroyo stones into the swimming pool below.

TOP RIGHT Basins plumbed with gas and filled with lava stones create the nighttime effect of floating fire.

RIGHT The vanishing edge of this infinity pool appears to merge with the Pacific Ocean.

OPPOSITE TOP The sleek, rectangular pool harmonizes with the boxy, modern lines of the house.

LEFT English designer Arabella Lennox-Boyd merged turf-paved steps with a stair-step waterfall that tumbles to a lower pond. Despite the streamlined look, this garden has its roots in traditional design, creating a pleasing tension.

the natural wonder of waterfalls

LEFT Dense foliage conceals the fact that this waterfall is built in one corner of a small suburban lot, abutting the property line.

ABOVE In this city garden, planters along the sides of the waterfall and stream soften the hard edges of the patio.

OPPOSITE While water lilies prefer to grow in still water, pickerell weed (*Pontederia cordata*) and water hyacinths (*Eichhornia crassipes*) thrive in the turbulence of the waterfall.

ABOVE A potting bench tucked at the bottom of the garden provides storage space for tools and pots.

LEFT The ogee arch gives this humble corner storage shed an air of architectural distinction.

RIGHT Swimming-pool equipment is stored gracefully out of sight behind these lattice walls.

OPPOSITE TOP Cleverly applied distressing and a few architectural details turns this outhouse into a whimsical garden feature.

in and out of sight

Let's face it: you need a spot to keep your tools. And while there's no question about their necessity, unconcealed trash cans can be quite unsightly. Create behind-the-scenes utility areas for pool chemicals and gardening paraphernalia. You can also build bench seating on your deck or patio that conceals ample storage space under the cushions.

bright idea

lawnmower storage

Look for "found" storage space under a deck or porch for bulky garden equipment.

bright idea

removable lath panels

In winter, the lath panels closest to the house are removed to let in more sunlight and warmth; in summer they are replaced to shade and cool the building.

trellises and lath lend cooling shade

ABOVE Lath is an inexpensive and effective way to filter sunlight.

LEFT Tools hang handily from the slats of this trellis, while plants twine between the spaces.

RIGHT Clematis 'William Kenneth' climbs up a trellis support.

OPPOSITE TOP LEFT Fragrant moonvines (*Ipomoea alba*) grow over a trellis arbor.

OPPOSITE TOP RIGHT Ivy trained in a trellis pattern adds texture to a bare wall.

OPPOSITE BOTTOM The trellis adds height to the wall and screens the far end of the garden from the driveway.

LEFT A dry stone wall complements a cottage-style garden. Here, lupines tower above *Geranium endressii* 'Wargrave Pink', and *Genista lydia* spread out in a golden mass.

BELOW The flower colors are echoed in a painted, zigzag retaining wall that doubles as a garden bench.

OPPOSITE LEFT A hollow wall makes an ideal planter for shallow rooted, drought-tolerant plants such as succulents and sedums. Spilling over the top, they soften the wall's hard edges.

brick walls on a budget

Serpentine walls (opposite bottom right) and pier-and-panel brick walls can be significantly less expensive to build than brick walls constructed by other methods. *Serpentine walls* get their lateral strength from their curves; pier-and-panel walls are braced by intermittent masonry piers and steel bars attached to the piers as reinforcement. In both cases, the walls can be half the thickness of a standard brick wall. *Pier-and-panel walls* can be built directly on the ground because foundations are required only under the piers. The savings on labor and materials is significant.

For specifications on building a serpentine or a pier-and-panel wall without footings under the panels, contact the Brick Industry Association. (See Resources, page 198.)

ABOVE Using a painting technique known as *trompe l'oeil* (French for "deceives the eye"), a skilled artist created the illusion of stone blocks on this stucco wall.

BELOW Thomas Jefferson incorporated serpentine walls into the architecture of the University of Virginia in 1824. Because their sinuous curves help to resist lateral forces, serpentine walls can be built in a single wythe (the thickness of one brick). This technique makes their construction more economical than straight brick walls, which would easily topple if they were that thin.

the living beauty of a garden wall

enhancing views and vistas

ABOVE LEFT The view across the pond is framed by the curved branch of the tree, trained when young to create this window.

ABOVE This path functions as an arrow pointing to the hilltop tower, emphasizing the borrowed view.

LEFT Trees in the foreground frame the view, allowing extra glimpses of the water between their trunks. The composition would be much less interesting if all the trees had been cut down.

OPPOSITE Using a plant training technique called "pleaching," the branches of golden chain trees (*Laburnum x watereri* 'Vossii') have been woven to form an arch.

RIGHT Grass paths accentuate the curved terrace walls. The sloped beds, planted with colored and textured evergreens as well as flowering perennials, look attractive all year.

BELOW A series of ponds on the terraced slope resemble pools in a rocky scree. Water circulates through the ponds by way of streams and waterfalls.

BOTTOM Dry stone walls follow the contour of the slope in a gentle curve, structuring the medley of plants spilling from beds and cropping up between pavers and stacked stones.

bright idea

scaling down

Take a grand idea, such as the terraced lawn at Middleton Place Plantation near Charleston, South Carolina, and adapt it to fit your own garden.

terraces add levels of interest

anatomy of a terraced slope

To create a series of level terraces on a slope, use the soil from the base of a retaining wall as the backfill behind the wall, as seen in the illustration below. If you prefer one large, level space, cut the slope in the spot where you want the wall, then use the excess soil to level the slope farther downhill.

To provide proper drainage, lay a perforated drainpipe behind the wall at the original ground level. Position the pipe with the drain holes facing down and the pipe sloping at least ¼ inch per foot so water moves away from the wall. Surround the pipe with gravel to keep out soil; then backfill. Alternatively, you can insert drainpipes through the lower part of the retaining wall every 32 inches so water can flow out of the front of the wall (right).

wood **o**ptions

- **Rot-resistant woods:** Redwood, cypress, and many cedar woods contain natural chemical compounds that repel bugs, bacteria, and other agents of decomposition. Other woods, such as white oak and black locust, provide physical barriers to rot by preventing moisture and decay-causing creatures from getting into the wood.
- **Pressure-treated lumber:** Wood is immersed in a liquid preservative (usually alkaline copper quat), and placed under pressure to force the chemical deep into the wood fibers.
- **Composite woods:** Made from recycled wood fibers, polymer trash bags, and recycled plastic bottles, composite wood is 30 to 50 percent more expensive than natural wood, but comes with a 10- to 20-year warranty.

places to perch

No landscape design is complete without a place to relax and enjoy the fruits of your labor. Patios and decks serve as outdoor rooms where family and friends can dine, play, and party. Benches, chaises, and other furniture provide comfortable spots for reading, chatting, or a quick afternoon nap. And while you are feathering your outdoor nest, consider the avian friends that share your space. Hang a seed-filled birdhouse on a sturdy tree branch, and you'll be rewarded with the cheerful songs of your favorite winged companions.

living off the ground

OPPOSITE TOP Deck boards are laid at angles to create an interesting pattern that draws the eye to the central birdbath.

OPPOSITE BOTTOM A series of deck levels is achieved by widening the landings. This creates additional seating and adds visual interest to the design.

ABOVE RIGHT Benches around the perimeter of the deck double as protective railings.

RIGHT Straddling the stream and overlooking the meadow, this deck provides a comfortable spot to relax and enjoy the great outdoors. The pale-blue wood stain creates a pleasing aged patina.

benches and furniture for taking in the view

OPPOSITE TOP A pair of Adirondack chairs are positioned to enjoy the view.

LEFT This stylized leaf chair and side table by Cricket Forge Garden Sculptures is in harmony with its bower-like setting.

OPPOSITE BOTTOM The upholstery on these synthetic wicker-and-rattan chairs is specially treated to be weatherproof. In the container, the lacy golden leaves of 'Tiger Eyes' Sumac (*Rhus typhina* 'Bailtiger' PPAF) provides a long season of interest.

TOP RIGHT This Chippendale-style bench echoes the colors of the flowers on the retaining wall.

MIDDLE RIGHT The development of steel production techniques in the eighteenth century made intricate furniture designs possible. Today's cast-aluminum furniture mimics the look without the weight or rust.

BOTTOM RIGHT The stone bench built into the hillside blends organically into the setting, looking as if had been there for eons.

fabric care

To keep outdoor fabric cushions clean, stack them indoors when not in use. When they do need washing, scrub them with mild detergent and water, rinse well, and set them on their sides to dry. Also set them on edge after a rain. Wet cushions are prone to mildew, and they may also pick up rust stains from metal furniture.

patios provide a retreat from summer sun

brick-pattern ideas

LEFT In a climate where the sun is reliably hot, a shaded patio is a welcome retreat. Here, a fluted canvas awning provides shelter and complements the modern design of the house.

ABOVE Brick laid in a freeform pattern appears to swirl and eddy like flowing water as the path opens up to form an informal private patio.

RIGHT The circle, arc, and sphere motif is repeated throughout this patio designed by Erik de Maeijer and Jane Hudson. Set away from the house, it is reached by round stepping stones.

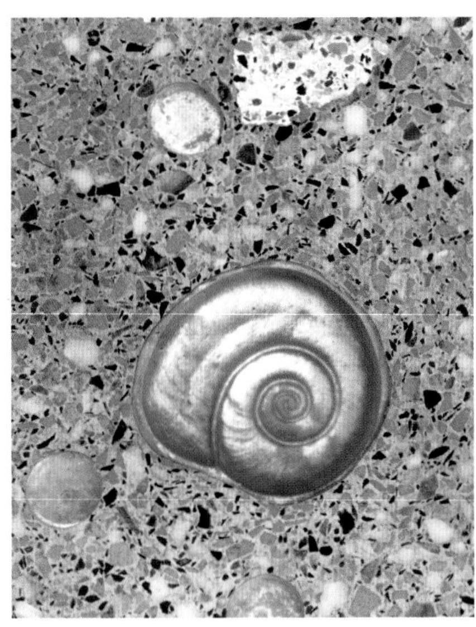

LEFT Pennsylvania bluestone cut in varying rectangles and squares lends a tailored look to this patio.

ABOVE Terrazzo is a composite material developed in fifteenth-century Italy that combines leftover marble and glass from mosaic installations. This terrazzo patio was created by fashion designer Zandra Rhodes.

OPPOSITE RIGHT Because the same terra-cotta tile paving was used both inside and outside, the eye is drawn without distraction to the vanishing-edge pool and the view beyond.

paving-stone options

Stone quarried locally generally will be less expensive than stone shipped great distances and will be more in harmony with the surroundings. Some stones, such as Tennessee sandstone and limestone, are more porous than others, making them more vulnerable to freeze-thaw cycles, which can cause them to flake and break. These porous stones are better suited to mild climates.

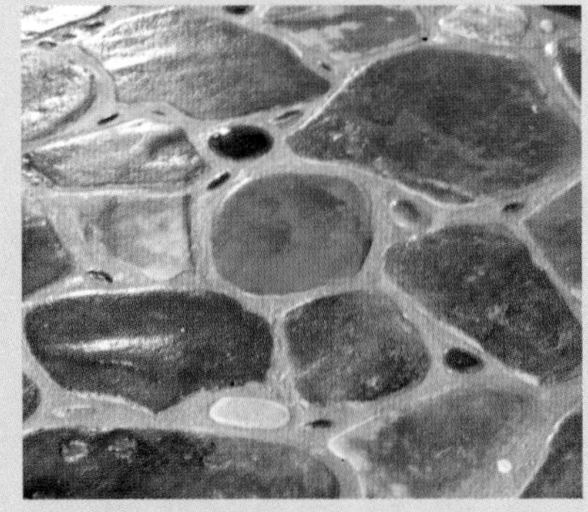

RIVER STONES

VERMONT SLATE

bright idea

merge indoors and outdoors

Using the same paving material indoors and outside visually enlarges both spaces.

TENNESSEE SANDSTONE

QUARTZITE FLAGSTONES

PENNSYLVANIA BLUESTONE

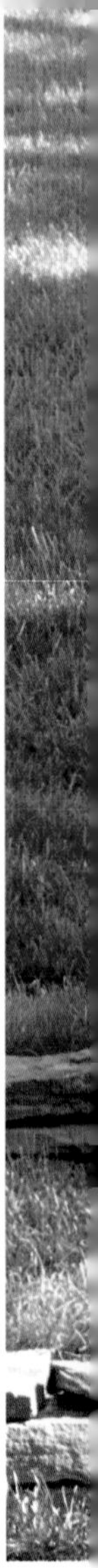

pampering our feathered friends

ABOVE The zinnia 'Zowie' blends well with the terra-cotta birdbath.

RIGHT Birds are very particular about the floor space and entrance-hole size of their houses. If the hole is too small, the birds may enlarge it themselves.

LEFT AND ABOVE LEFT Each bird species has its own food preferences. Sunflower seeds, millet, and cracked corn are popular with many birds. High-fat snacks such as suet, peanut butter, bacon drippings, and shortening are energy-filled foods that help birds perform optimally.

ABOVE RIGHT As long as the interior is clean, the floor space inside is the desired dimensions, and the entrance hole is the right diameter, the nesting birds will overlook the cat-that-got-the canary motif of their home.

the benefits of birds

Besides being fun to watch, birds play an important role in providing insect control in the garden. Barn swallows and purple martins eat pounds of mosquitoes and other flying insects in a day, as do starling and titmouse nestlings. Sparrows and goldfinches gobble up aphids. Wrens will feed each of their fledglings as many as 500 insects in an afternoon, while a brown thrasher eats as many as 6,800 insects in 24 hours. As any home gardener knows, birds alone don't control insect pests; however, they are part of the complex ecosystem and play an important role in the balance. To attract birds to your garden, provide for their basic necessities: food, water, comfortable nesting spots, and cover from predators.

7

It's no secret that different regions of the country present their own unique climate challenges. But even the smallest plot may be affected by a variety of different growing environments, known as "microclimates." For example, a low-lying area on one side of your home may be swampy after a rain; in another section of your landscape, a heavy canopy of trees might create deep, dry shade. The wise gardener learns to work with the site, using plants that tolerate the conditions at hand. Quite often, a creative adaptation to a tricky habitat can transform a garden problem into a garden triumph.

Garden Habitats

- lofty elevations
- humid climates
- wooded locales
- urban and desert oases

Tall trees are "limbed up" (stripped of their lower branches) to allow enough light for growing a collection of shade-loving shrubs and flowers.

lofty elevations

Celebrate lofty elevations and the unique features they bring to your garden. Carve a terrace with spectacular views from a slope behind your home or create a zigzag path that traverses a hillside. A roof garden can add more living space to a city dwelling and provide a welcome patch of greenery to the urban landscape.

LEFT Yucca filamentosa is a spiky focal point amidst fountain grass, artemesia, and juniper.

ABOVE A small patio was carved out of this slope. The retaining wall of railroad ties was inexpensive to build.

BELOW Impatiens provide nearly year-round color on this Southern California hillside. Shrubs and palm trees help anchor the design.

OPPOSITE Railroad ties used as stairs follow the contours of the slope.

create a garden on a curving slope

LEFT On a private rooftop, there is less concern about potential theft of valuable art, such as this mask propped against the planter.

BELOW The rooftop of the American Society of Landscape Architects (ASLA) headquarters in Washington, D.C., features a selection of drought-tolerant plants that create a prairie effect.

OPPOSITE TOP When properly reinforced, a roof can hold the weight of a raised pond. Here, the edge of the pond doubles as a seat.

OPPOSITE BOTTOM The roof of this garden shed is planted with drought-tolerant, shallow-rooted succulents. Sedums and ice plants (var. *Delosperma*) are ideal green-roof inhabitants.

rooftop gardens

what is a **g**reen **r**oof?

The term "green roof" refers to the top of a home or public building that is covered in rooted, growing plants. The concept dates back to ancient Mesopotamia and has been in various stages of development in Europe and Scandinavia for many decades. However, the movement is just getting started in the United States, where two of the country's best-known green roofs are atop Chicago's City Hall and a Ford Motor Co. facility in Dearborn, Michigan.

Studies have shown that green roofs can absorb nearly half the water that would otherwise drain away after a rain, while also cutting summer rooftop temperatures by up to 30 percent. Other environmental benefits of green roofs include

- Providing insulation to reduce the building's heating and cooling loads
- Increasing a roof's life span
- Filtering pollutants and carbon dioxide out of the air

The garden shed roof, right, is an example of an extensive green roof, a lightweight category of green roof that features a shallow planting-medium depth of six inches or less. The soilless medium is placed on top of a waterproof membrane.

humid climates

Salty, damp breezes and sandy soil make seaside gardening a challenge, but the rewards make the effort worthwhile. Find out what varieties other gardeners in your area are growing with success. In frost-free regions, brightly colored tropical foliage and flowers add lush drama. While most varieties cannot survive winter freezes, tropical plants do thrive during the hot, humid summers that occur in most regions of North America.

wet ground can be a growing opportunity

OPPOSITE Swamp pinks (*Helonias bullata*), primroses, ferns, and wild sweet William (*Phlox divaricata*) thrive along this moist stream bank.

ABOVE Many canna lily varieties flourish when planted in or near water.

RIGHT Water-loving plants include the fragrant primrose (*Primula florindae*), sidalcia, astilbe, forget-me-nots, and *Ligularia stenocephala* 'The Rocket'.

bright idea

seaside theme

Celebrate life on the water with nautical garden ornaments and accents.

gardens by the sea

TOP LEFT Fountain grass (*Pennisetum alopecuroides*) adapts well to the sandy soil and salty air.

LEFT The terrazzo paving design by Zandra Rhodes enlivens this ocean-view garden, planted with New Zealand flax (*Phormium tenax*).

BELOW Abalone shells set into the rounded end of the stone wall lend an aquatic accent.

OPPOSITE This pelican sculpture fits perfectly with the seaside setting.

OPPOSITE Palms and ferns combine in a lush tropical planting that surrounds this front-garden pond.

TOP Caladiums such as the multicolored 'Carolyn Wharton' may be planted as annuals in cold-season gardens. They add bright tropical color and marry well with cold-hardy foliage plants.

RIGHT Unlike most Mandevillas, 'Red Riding Hood' doesn't vine, making it ideal for hanging baskets. In warm climates it flowers all year.

BELOW An Australian tree fern spreads like an umbrella over the hammock, providing shade and a whispering sound when a breeze rustles the enormous fronds.

luxuriant tropical gardens

TOP Shade-loving rhododendron are planted as the understory layer in this woodland garden, while hostas and ferns make a dense ground cover.

ABOVE Shrub-filled beds flourish in the filtered light of a high canopy woodland. Good candidates for this environment include *Pieris japonica*, azalea, red osier dogwood (*Cornus sericea*), aucuba, holly, and beautyberry.

RIGHT This wide-bark path creates an avenue through the dogwood trees, giving structure to the woodland setting without spoiling the natural look.

wooded locales

The special microclimate created by shade can grow a wide assortment of plants. Whether it is provided by a single large specimen tree, a wooded area, or a building, shade can be a welcome escape from direct sun and heat. Yet even shade lovers need some light. An area in full shade that is bright will support a wider variety of plants than a spot that gets an hour or two of direct sun but is very dark the rest of the day. Be aware of how bright your wooded or shady area is, and choose plants accordingly.

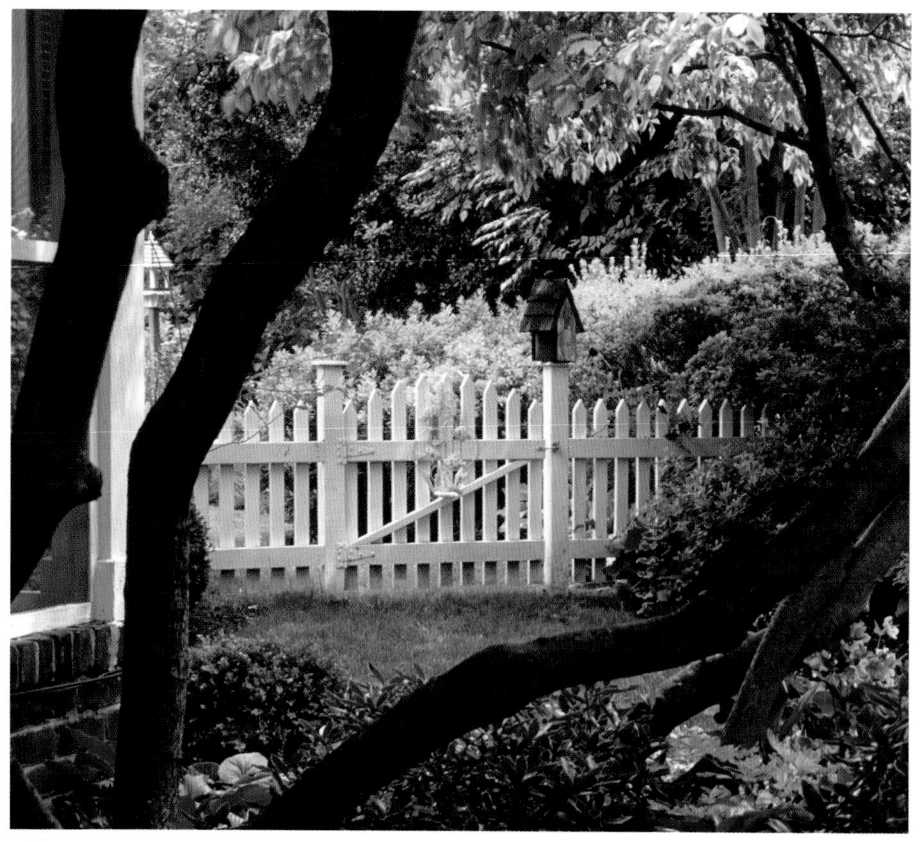

LEFT The lower branches of this multistemmed tree have been pruned to reveal an interesting pattern, as well as to provide enough sunlight for additional shrubbery to grow underneath.

BELOW Cyclamen, daffodils, and other early-flowering bulbs that require full sun do well when planted under deciduous trees and shrubs; they will flower before the new leaves overshadow them.

OPPOSITE A stepping-stone path and lush ferns, deadnettle, and other shade lovers planted in this dark space between the house and property line transform a problem area into an alluring spot.

shade-loving landscapes

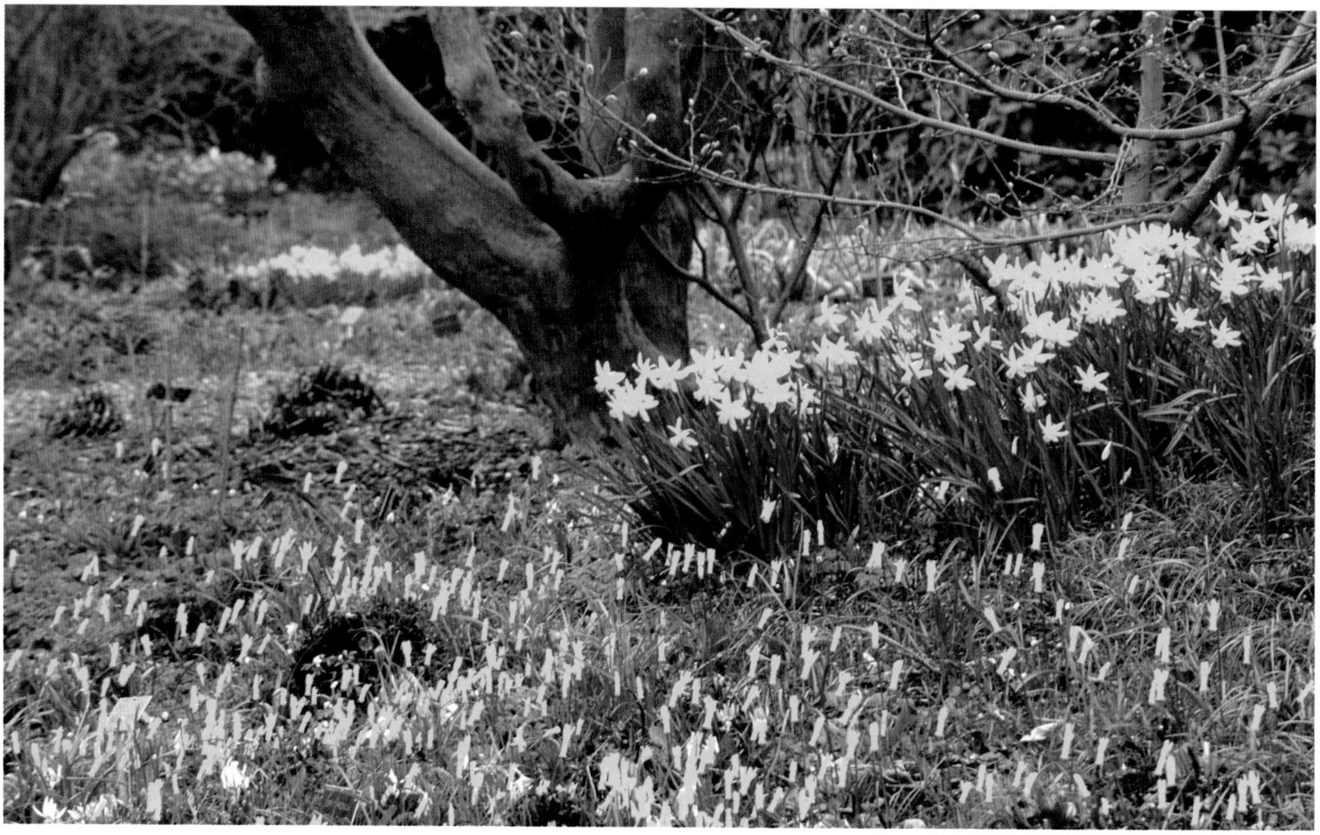

rocks and plants make striking counterpoints

OPPOSITE Traditional alpine plants don't thrive in most regions of North America. Instead, this rock garden is filled with easy-care plants such as Russian sage, fountain grass, and Joe-Pye weed.

ABOVE Native boulders left in place create the framework for this dry-slope rock garden in California. Pincushion protea (*Leucospermum cordifolium*), a good choice for nutrient-poor soil, echoes the rocks' rounded shape.

TOP RIGHT *Crocus vernus albiflorus* both complements and contrasts with the sculptural stone set on its end.

RIGHT Small plants, including hosta, saxifrage, and primroses grace this rock garden and waterfall.

meadow plantings

OPPOSITE TOP A path cut through the tall grass creates an enchanting design and lends access to the meadow.

OPPOSITE BOTTOM LEFT This natural-looking meadow planting features a whimsical boxwood topiary as a focal point.

OPPOSITE BOTTOM RIGHT Daffodils are excellent for meadow plantings because they can push through thick turf to emerge. These flowers need to retain their foliage to store energy for next year's blooms, so do not mow them.

LEFT This mortared-stone retaining wall follows the natural contour of the land, creating an undulating wave effect. The wall's irregular shape also serves as a transition between the wild meadow and the paved driveway area.

creating a meadow

Establishing a meadow can be a labor-intensive operation. One fairly easy technique is to first cover existing plantings with a thick layer of newspaper to smother any unwanted plants and weeds. Next, pile on approximately eight inches of topsoil; then water until thoroughly damp. Cover with a tarpaulin for several weeks. When it is time to plant, remove the tarpaulin. Choose either a seed mixture or a variety of forb plugs (a forb is any broad-leaved plant that isn't a tree, shrub, or grass) suited to your region.

Wildflower meadows require mowing to allow more desirable species to flourish and to reduce the vigor of the more rampant species. Spring flower meadows should be left unmown from late fall through July, and then mown regularly to a height of two to three inches. Wait until late August or September to mow summer-flower meadows. Instead of collecting the clippings immediately, leave them in place for a few days after mowing to allow seed to drop.

A new meadow needs to be weeded and watered regularly for two to three years to give desired plants a chance to establish themselves. It will take as many as seven years for the meadow to be fully established, evolving from the annuals that dominate in the first year, to biennials and annuals in the second, and ultimately to perennials.

vary by region and growing conditions

RIGHT An urn positioned midway down the brick path that runs through this urban garden minimizes the perception of the spaces's narrow dimensions.

urban and desert oases

Too hot, too dry, too rocky, too exposed, too cramped: These apparent bothers can be turned into bonuses by creating a specialty garden that thrives under the extreme conditions of your area. For example, a desert oasis might feature succulents that are rich in texture and color, and other drought-tolerant plants that erupt in unexpectedly delicate flowers after a winter rain. Whether you plant flowering annuals in containers or add trellised vines to a bare wall, a garden in the city can become an essential retreat from the bustle of traffic and people.

city greenery

OPPOSITE LEFT There is space in this city garden for a demi-lune-shape patio and lawn. The repeating arc lends unity to the design.

RIGHT In this side garden, raised beds and trellised vines enliven a long stretch of wall and carry floral interest to eye level.

bright idea

brighten with white

In a shady garden, use white flowers or silver foliage to lighten the space.

LEFT *Acacia redolens* provides the backbone for this desert garden planting. The silver foliage of artemesia 'Powis Castle' complements the acacia, while fortnight lily (*Dietes bicolor*) adds spiky texture.

BELOW The ground cover Gazania 'Sundrop' is punctuated with spiky *Agave victoriae-reginae*.

RIGHT In winter, succulents such as this aloe 'David Verity' make a dramatic display.

refreshing desert gardens

bright idea

lawn substitutes

Using drought-tolerant ground covers such as ice plants, gazanias, or sedum instead of turf grass is both economical and environmentally friendly.

OPPOSITE FAR LEFT Firecracker cactus (*Cleistocactus baumannii*) is one of hundreds of cacti family members.

LEFT Drought-tolerant succulents and cacti provide wonderful colors and textures in the desert garden.

8

It's the clever gardener who recognizes that a well-planned landscape can—and should—be beautiful, not only during the brief weeks when trees and plants are in full bloom but throughout the entire year. Organizing a four-season garden is easy to do once you begin. The key is to select plants that maintain interest for several seasons. For example, many ornamental grasses produce attractive seed heads and dried stalks that shine in the winter sun. By adding a few of these essential elements to your landscape design, you will find something to delight your senses even on the dreariest of winter days.

Seasonal Gardens

- nature's rhythms
- spring awakening
- summer blooms
- autumn color
- winter landscapes

Goldenrod, asters, and sedum 'Autumn Joy' offer a bright farewell before winter. Other fall choices include dahlias, hardy ageratum, and, of course, chrysanthemums.

nature's rhythms

In spring, early buds herald the start of the growing season. As the sun grows hot, annuals and perennials burst with bold color. Brilliant foliage and berries are autumn's parting gifts before the spare beauty of winter arrives.

the sap rises and life is renewed

ABOVE Thousands of snowdrops have naturalized in this woodland garden. Snowdrops self-sow readily and will flower even when there is snow on the ground.

LEFT An arc of red-flowering azaleas defines the border between woodland and cultivated garden.

OPPOSITE Tulips, blue Spanish bluebells (*Scilla campanulata*), and wild columbine (*Aquilegia canadensis*) are combined in this spring garden.

LEFT The arbor over this small patio creates a shady bower for informal entertaining.

RIGHT Annuals such as impatiens, ageratum, and wax begonias provide summer-long color.

OPPOSITE FAR RIGHT A water feature offers cooling refreshment during hot summer days.

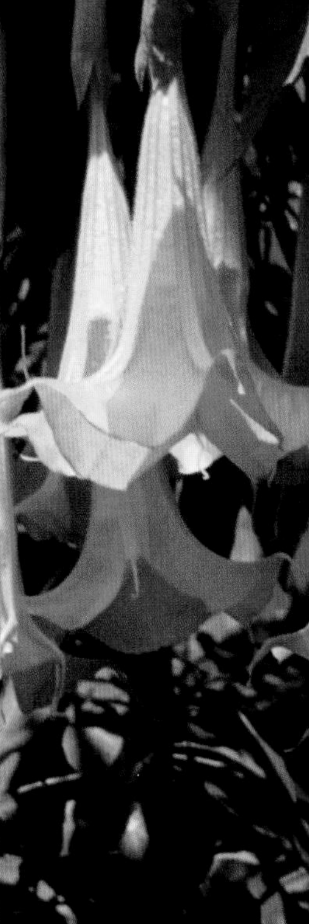

RIGHT Angel's trumpets thrive in summer temperatures. In colder climates, overwinter them indoors.

OPPOSITE FAR RIGHT This arbor defines the pool area, framing the view through its arches.

bright idea

absentee watering

Cluster all your plant containers and position a hose-end sprinkler equipped with an automatic timer so that water falls on all the plants while you're away.

summertime, and the living is easy

RIGHT An avenue of goldenrain trees (*Koelreuteria paniculata*) provides four seasons of interest: structure in the winter, new growth in spring, clusters of yellow flowers in summer, and dramatic autumn foliage.

BELOW Japanese anemone (*Anemone hupehensis* var. *japonica*) stars in the autumn garden. Here the hybrid 'Bressingham Glow' looks ready to escape the confines of the boxwood hedge.

BELOW RIGHT Dried ornamental grasses and seed heads provide a special beauty late in the year. Structure becomes especially important when flowers have died and the garden is fading.

the mellow harvest season

BELOW The crocus-like flowers and dark-green leaves of Colchicum provide a fresh, springlike splash of color in this autumn garden.

bright idea

mulch leaves

Use a mulching mower to shred fallen leaves. Spread the leaves on your beds or pile them on the compost heap.

the spare beauty of a shapely branch

ABOVE A garden built on the structure provided by hedges, paths, and walls will provide greater interest in winter.

RIGHT Witch hazel 'Primavera' is an upright, vase-shaped cultivar with fragrant blossoms that open in February and March.

OPPOSITE BOTTOM LEFT With its bold, red bark, Redtwig dogwood (*Cornus alba* 'Sibirica') sets the winter landscape

LEFT *Pieris japonica*, an evergreen shrub hardy in USDA zones 5–8, flowers for several weeks in early spring.

CENTER LEFT Heavenly bamboo (*Nandina domestica*) produces large clumps of berries that hold well into spring.

BELOW The coral bark maple ('Senkaki') makes a dramatic impact on this winter landscape. It prefers even moisture and a slightly acid, well-drained soil.

Resource Guide

ASSOCIATIONS

American Society of Landscape Architects (ASLA)

202-898-2444

www.asla.org

National professional organization that represents landscape architects. ASLA provides information online for professionals and the general public.

American Nursery & Landscape Association (ANLA)

202-789-2900

www.anla.org

National organization of the nursery and landscape industry. Members grow, distribute, and retail plants, and design and install landscapes for residential and commercial customers.

Mr. Smarty Plants

Lady Bird Johnson Wildflower Center

512-232-0100

www.wildflower.org/expert

Resource for information pertaining to landscaping with wildflowers

The Brick Industry Association (BIA)

703-620-0010

www.brickinfo.org

National trade association that represents distributors and manufacturers of clay brick and suppliers of related products and services. BIA provides information online for professionals and the general public.

The Fertilizer Institute

202-962-0490

www.tfi.org

Provides information about fertilizer use for healthy, bountiful plants

PRODUCTS

Clean Air Gardening

214-363-5170

www.cleanairgardening.com

Retail source for environmentally friendly lawn and garden supplies

Earl May

www.earlmay.com

Retail source for long-lasting, quality landscaping equipment and products, including precut limestone, fertilizer, and soil

Gardenscape

www.gardenscape.on.ca

Sells garden items to gardeners in the U.S. and Canada

The following list of manufacturers and associations is meant to be a general guide to industry and product-related sources. It is not intended as a listing of products and manufacturers represented by the photographs in this book.

Garden Supplies Guide

www.gardeningsuppliesguide.com

Online guide to a variety of suppliers of garden-tool manufacturers

Home, Garden, and Patio Outlet

913-422-7792.

www.homegardenandpatio.com

Retail source for home, garden, and patio furniture and decor, as well as landscaping tools and products

Landscape USA

www.landscapeusa.com

800-966-1033

Sells landscaping, irrigation, and gardening supplies

Park Seed

800-213-0076

www.parkseed.com

A retail source of seeds for American gardens, including everything needed to start your own seeds at home

Seeds of Change

888-762-7333

www.seedsofchange.com

Offers everything from seeds to gardening tools and strives to help preserve biodiversity and promote sustainable, organic agriculture

PUBLIC GARDENS

Buffalo Springs Herb Garden

7 Kennedy-Wade's Mill Loop

Raphine, VA 24472

540-348-1083

www.buffaloherbs.com

Chanticleer Garden

786 Church Rd.

Wayne, PA 19087

610-687-4163

www.chanticleergarden.org

Dumbarton Oaks

1703 32nd St., NW

Washington, D.C. 20007

202-339-6401

www.doaks.org

The New York Botanical Gardens

Bronx River Pkwy. at Fordham Rd.

Bronx, NY 10458

718-817-8700

www.nybg.org

Glossary

Acidic: A pH measure less than 7 (neutral), indicating a low level of hydrogen.

Aggregate: Crushed stone, gravel, or other material added to cement to make concrete or mortar.

Alkaline: A pH measure above 7 (neutral), indicating a high level of hydrogen.

Apex (plural: apices): The tip (tips) of branches or the end buds of a growing plant.

Arbor: An arched, open structure that spans a doorway or provides shelter for a seat.

Arborize: Pruning overgrown shrubs to a primary stem so that they resemble small trees.

Ashlar: Stone cut at a quarry to produce smooth, flat bedding surfaces that stack easily. Walls made from such stones have a formal appearance.

BT (Bacillus thuringiensis): A microbe that is toxic to caterpillars, but that is harmless to birds, mammals, bees, and other insects. Sold commercially as an organic pest control product.

Backfill: To fill in an area, such as a planting hole, trench, or around a foundation, using soil or gravel.

Base map: A drawing or survey that details the location of all property boundaries, structures, slopes, significant plantings, and location of sunrise and sunset. An important first step in landscaping.

Bat: A brick cut in half lengthwise.

Batten: A cross-piece used to reinforce a gate or door.

Bed joint: Horizontal masonry joint, as opposed to a vertical masonry joint (called a head joint).

Beneficials: Animals, microbes, and insects—such as ladybugs, parasitic wasps, and hoverflies—that prey upon garden pests.

Berm: A mound of earth that directs or retains water.

Bond: The arrangement of bricks that creates a pattern in a wall or other masonry structure.

Bond stones: Support stones that extend through the full thickness of a wall. They are staggered and placed every few feet along the length of the wall for extra strength.

Bud: An unopened cluster of leaves or of a flower, where growth occurs.

Butyl synthetic rubber flexible liner: A very durable material used to line ponds.

Cap: The top, flat layer of a masonry structure. (Also Coping.)

Catch basin: An underground reservoir to collect excess water. Usually located in the lowest part of the garden.

Circuit: A system for watering small, designated areas rather than an entire area at once.

Clay: Soil that consists of extremely fine particles that pack together tightly, so that water drains through slowly.

Collar: The slight swelling that occurs where a branch of a tree or shrub meets the trunk. (Also Saddle.)

Collar joint: The vertical joint between two stacks of bricks or stones.

Commons: The cheapest grade of bricks; for all-purpose building.

Computer-assisted design programs (CAD): Computer programs that allow homeowners to design their own landscapes without the effort of drawing on paper.

Concrete bonder: A material applied to concrete block to help stucco adhere to the surface.

Course: A horizontal row of bricks or stones.

Cover crops: Crops, such as clover, annual rye, vetch, barley, and buckwheat, used to blanket the ground and choke out weeds.

Crown: Where the upper part of the plant joins the roots, usually at soil level.

Cultivar: Short for cultivated variety. A plant variety developed in cultivation, rather than occurring naturally in the wild.

Diatomaceous earth: A mineral created from the fossilized remains of ancient marine creatures.

Double dig: A method for improving soil at a deeper level than usual. Dig a trench, loosen and amend the soil at the bottom of the trench; and then backfill with amended topsoil.

Drip irrigation: A system that delivers water at a slow rate directly to plant roots.

Drip line: An imaginary line in the soil around a tree or shrub that mirrors the circumference of the canopy above.

Dry-laid walk: A masonry path installed without mortar.

Dry wall: A stone wall that does not contain mortar.

Emitter: Water delivery device on a drip irrigation system.

Engineering brick: Top-grade brick. The hardest and most impervious to weathering.

English bond: A brick pattern that contains periodic headers in each course, adding strength to the wall.

EPDM: Ethylene Propylene Diene Monomer; an extremely durable and flexible rubber material used for lining ponds.

Facing brick: A type of brick used when consistency in appearance is required.

Flemish bond: A brick pattern that alternates courses of headers with stretchers, adding strength to the wall.

Float: A steel, aluminum, or wood object used to smooth the surface of poured concrete by driving large aggregate below the surface.

Floater: A plant that grows on the surface of water and draws its nutrients from water, rather than from soil.

Footing: The concrete base that supports a masonry wall or other structure.

Footprint: The perimeter of a house or other significant structures, shown on a property survey.

Friable: Refers to a soil texture that is crumbly and easy to work, such as with loam.

Garden room: Outdoor space bordered by hedges, trellises, or constructed walls, creating a sense of privacy or seclusion.

Genus (plural: genera): A closely related group of species sharing similar characteristics and probably evolved from the same ancestors.

Green manure: A cover crop grown and turned or plowed under the soil to improve its texture and nutrient content.

Growth bud: Usually the tip or end bud of a branch, where growth chemicals are concentrated.

Hardiness: A plant's ability to survive winter cold or summer heat without protection.

Glossary

Hardscape: Parts of a landscape constructed from materials other than plants, such as walks, walls, and trellises, made of wood, stone, or other materials.

Hardware cloth: A flexible, wire mesh. Sometimes used to roughen a base coat of stucco.

Hardwood cutting: The removal of pencil-thick tips of branches (5 to 8 inches long) at the end of the growing season when the wood has completely hardened. The cuttings are rooted, then planted outdoors.

Headers: Bricks turned horizontal to the stretcher courses.

Heeling in: Planting bare-root stock in a temporary but protected location, with the trunk tilted on a sharp diagonal to discourage rooting.

Heirloom vegetables: Plants grown from seed that has been collected and saved over many generations.

Humus: Decayed organic material rich with nutrients. Its spongy texture holds moisture.

Inflorescense: The "flower" of an ornamental grass. A cluster of seeds which is borne on top of the grass blade.

Interplanting: To combine plants with different bloom times or growth habits, making it possible to fit more plants in a bed, thus prolonging the bed's appeal.

IPM: Integrated Pest Management. An approach to pest control that utilizes regular monitoring to determine if and when control is needed.

Jointing: The finish given to the mortar that extrudes from each course of bricks.

Landscape fabric: A synthetic fabric, sometimes water-permeable, spread under paths or mulch to serve as a weed barrier.

Lateral branch: A side branch that connects to the trunk or primary branch of a tree or shrub.

Limbing up: Pruning a tree's lower branches as high as 30 to 40 feet to allow more light to reach lawn and plants below.

Loam: An ideal soil for gardening, containing plenty of organic matter and a balanced range of small to large mineral particles.

Marginal plants: Plants that grow around the edges of water bodies; their roots are submerged while their leaves and flowers are above the surface of the water.

Microclimate: Small area with unique growing conditions, usually as a result of a land formation (such as a valley or pond) or nearby structure (such as a building or stone wall).

Monoculture: The practice of growing only one type of plant in a given area.

Node: The area of a stem where leaf growth occurs.

Organic matter: Plant and animal debris, such as leaves, garden trimmings, and manure, in various stages of decomposition.

Overwinter: To keep a marginally hardy plant alive during the winter so that it can resume growth the following spring.

Oxygenator: Underwater plants that absorb nutrients and carbon dioxide from fish wastes and decaying materials, thus helping to starve out algae.

Parterre: Diminutive hedges, such as boxwood, used to divide space and serve as decorative frames for other plantings in formal gardens.

Pathogen: A disease-causing agent.

Pergola: A tunnel-like walkway or seating area with columns or posts to support an open "roof" of beams or trelliswork. (Also Gallery.)

Pinching: Removing the growing tips of branches or shoots to encourage lush, bushy growth.

Plat: Prepared by professional surveyors, it shows precise property lines and any easements.

Polyethylene: A material used as a lining for temporary pools.

PVC: Polyvinyl Chloride. Material used for irrigation pipes; also used to make flexible pond liners.

PVC-E: A stronger and more flexible version of standard PVC.

Reinforcing rod: Steel bar inside the concrete foundation of a wall, used for extra support.

Rooting hormone powder: A substance applied to the end of a cutting to promote the growth of roots.

Semiripe: Neither new growth nor mature growth; cuttings taken from branches in early summer for the purpose of starting new plants.

Silt (silty): Soil that is sedimentary and fine in texture, but coarser than clay. It feels slippery and compacts easily.

Single dig: To excavate or turn soil to the depth of the head of the shovel or spade.

Soap: A brick cut to half its width.

Softscape: The palette of plants used in a landscape, as opposed to the hardscape, which refers to nonliving landscape objects, such as paths, stones, patios, and walls.

Softwood cutting: Growing tips (at least 3 to 4 inches long) of branches removed in late spring before growth has fully hardened, used for starting new plants.

Species: Among plants, a group that shares many characteristics, including essential flower types, and that can interbreed freely.

Sphagnum moss: A moisture-absorbent, partially decomposed plant material harvested from bogs and sold commercially as a soil amendment.

Stack bond: The arrangement of bricks in which mortar joints are not bridged by courses above and below. The weakest bond.

Stretchers: Bricks laid horizontally in the direction of the wall.

Synthetic rubber: The most durable and most expensive material used for pond liners. Two types: EPDM and butyl.

Tilth: Soil with an easy-to-work texture which is the result of a balanced mix of small and large particles and plenty of organic matter.

Topdress: To cover the surface of soil with a thin layer of compost or fertilizer.

Underplant: To plant low-growing plants, such as ground covers, under taller plants such as shrubs.

Vista: An avenue or line of sight that allows a distant view.

Weep holes: Holes that allow water to seep through a retaining wall so that it does not build up behind the wall.

Wythe: A vertical section of a wall that is equal to the width of the masonry unit.

Xeriscape: Landscape design that utilizes drought-tolerant plants and techniques for minimizing water use.

Zones: Climate divisions on a map indicating extreme cold or heat for that area, used to determine a plant's suitability.

Index

* Numbers in ***bold italic*** indicate pages with photos or illustrations.

A

Abalone shells, ***172***
Acacia redolens, ***186***
Accents
  armillary spheres as, 135
  birdbaths as, 162
  bird houses as, 162
  brick patterns as, 159
  container gardening and, 128–129
  espalier as, 130–131
  fencing as, 114–117
  follies as, 119
  garden pathways as, 120–127
  gates as, 116–117
  patios as, 155–161
  paving stones as, 161
  as structural statements, 112–113
  sundials as, 135
  terraced slopes as, 153
  terraces as, 152–153
  water features as, 136–144
  wood options as, 154
Acer palmatum 'Senkaki' (coral bark maple), ***197***
Achillea, ***22***
Adirondack chairs, ***156***
Agapanthus, ***61***
Agastache x *rupestris*, ***23***
Ageratum, ***20***, 189, ***193***
Allées, ***40***
Allium, 13, ***37***, ***94***
  'Purple Sensation', ***98***
Allium aflatunense, ***21***, ***63***
Aloe 'David Verity', ***187***
Alpine plants, ***180***
Alyssum, ***59***
American design
  Arts and Crafts, 32–33, 48, 52–53
  Colonial, 48, 49
  Victorian, 48, 50
American regional styles, 54–63
  Asian and English gardens, ***63–64***
  California-style garden, ***61***
  Midwest garden, ***55***
  Northeast garden, 56
  Pacific Northwest garden, ***62***
  South garden, ***57–58***
  Southwest garden, ***59***
  West Coast garden, ***60***
Analogous relationships, 23
Anemone hupehensis var. *japonica* (Japanese anemone), ***194***
Angel's trumpets, ***99***, ***193***
Annuals, ***37***, ***193***
Ante room, ***68***
Aquilegia canadensis (wild columbine), ***191***
Arbor, 112, ***112***, ***192***, ***193***
Arborvitae, ***43***
Armillary spheres, ***135***
Artemesia, ***166***
  'Powis Castle', ***186***
Assets, turning problems into, 132
Asters, 189
Astilbe, ***171***
Aucuba, ***176***
Australian tree fern, ***175***
Autumn gardens, 194–195
Axial rill, ***41***
Azaleas, ***19***, ***62***, ***176***, ***190***

B

Barberry, ***20***
Base map
  beginning with, 25
  recording information on, 24
Beautyberry, ***176***
Bedding out, 36
Beds, raised, ***185***
Benches, 110–111, ***155***
  Chippendale-style, ***157***
  stone, ***157***
Birdbaths, 162
Bird houses, 162
Bird of paradise (*Strelitzia nicolai*), ***97***
Birds
  food preferences for, 163
  in insect control, 163
Black-eyed Susan (*Rudbeckia fulgida* 'Goldsturm'), ***55***
Blue Atlas cedar, ***131***
Bollard lights, 92
Borders
  depth of, ***16***
  perennial, 36
Bougainvillaea, ***130***
Boxwood, ***18***, ***97***, ***107***
  as topiary, ***182***
Brick path, ***78***
Brick patterns, ***159***
Brick walls, 148
Broccoli, ***108***
Brush cherry (*Eugenia myrtifolia*), ***129***
Budget, preparing, 30
Bulbs, 126

C

Cabbages, ***94***, ***108***, ***109***
Cacti, ***59***, ***61***, ***187***
Caladium, 'Carolyn Wharton', ***175***
Caliche, 59
California garden, ***54***
Canna lily, ***99***, ***171***
Carpet bedding, 36
Cast aluminum furniture, ***157***
Cedar of Lebanon tree, ***106***
Centranthus rubra (red valerian), ***148***
Ceratopteris plumbagi noides (Plumbago), ***56***
Chinese gardens, ***34***, ***35***
Chinese zigzag bridges, ***35***
Chippendale-style bench, ***157***
Chippendale-style bridge, ***120***
Chrysanthemums, 189
Cleisto-cactus baumannii (firecracker cactus), ***186***
Clematis 'William Kenneth', ***147***
Climbing rose 'Seagull', ***99***
Colchicum, ***195***
Coleus, ***31***
  'Copper Glow', ***128***
  'Sedona', 23
Colonial gardens, 48, 49
Color, putting to work, 22
Color kinships, 23
Color Schemes for the Flower Garden (Jekyll), 97
Color-themed gardens, 98–99
Columbine, ***98***
Complementary relationships, 23
Composite woods, 154
Compost heap, ***195***
Container gardening, ***128–129***
Contoured fences, 114, ***115***
Coral bark maple (*Acer palmatum* 'Senkaki'), ***197***
Cordyline 'Red Star', ***129***
Cornus alba
  'Elegantissima', ***99***
  'Sibirica' (redtwig dogwood), ***197***
Cornus sericea (red osier dogwood), ***176***
Costs, cutting, 30
Cotinus coggyria pur pureau (smoke tree), ***23***
Creeping fig (*Ficus pumila*), ***103***
Creeping thyme, ***96***, ***134***
Crocus, 126
Crocus vernus albiflorus, ***181***
Curry plant (*Helichrysum italicum*), ***16***
Cyclamen, ***178***

D

Daffodils, 126, ***178***, ***183***
Dahlias, 189
Datura inoxia, ***99***
Daylilies, ***99***
Deadnettle, ***179***
Decks, 155–161
Desert oases, 184–187
Design principles, 12–23
  boxwood, 18
  color kinships, 23
  harmony and unity, 14–15
  light and shadow, 17
  mass and space, 18
  pond, 18
  proportion and scale, 16
  putting color to work, 22
  repetition, 15
  textures for visual variety, 20
  using landscape patterns, 19

Dietes bicolor (Fortnight lily), ***186***
Dogwood, ***177***
red osier (*Cornus sericea*), ***176***
redtwig (*Cornus alba* 'Sibirica'), ***197***
Double-complementary relationships, 23
Dry streambeds, ***24***
Dusty Millers, ***51***

E

Elder 'Sutherland Gold', ***99***
English gardens, ***34***, ***36–37***
Eratosthenes, ***135***
Espalier, ***130–131***
Eugenia myrtifolia (brush cherry), ***129***
Evergreens, ***42***

F

False cypress 'Sungold', ***99***
False olive (*Phillyrea angustifolia*), ***104–105***
Fences, 111
choices for slopes, 114–117
contoured, 114, ***115***
ironwork, 115
sloped, 114, ***115***
split-rail, ***114***
stepped, 114
Ferns, ***171***, ***174***, ***176***, ***179***
Fibonacci, Leonardo, 16
Fibonacci sequence, 16
Ficus pumila (creeping fig), ***103***
Firecracker cactus (*Cleisto-cactus baumannii*), ***186***
Fire pit, ***71***
Flagstones
for patio, ***28***
paving with, 77
quartzite, ***161***
Flanders poppies (*Papaver rhoeas*), 111
Flexible pond liners, 138
Floodlights, 82, ***84***, 92
Focal points, 111
Folly, 119
Forget-me-nots, ***171***
Fortnight lily (*Dietes bicolor*), ***186***
Foundation plantings, bed depth for, ***16***
Fountain grass (*Pennisetum alopecuroides*), ***166***, ***172***, ***180***
Fountains, 111, ***137***
raised, ***29***
recessing heads of, ***137***
Four-o'clocks, ***99***
Four-season garden, 189
Foxglove, ***99***
Foxtail lilies, ***37***
French aesthetic gardens, ***34***, ***40***
Front gardens, ***78–79***
pond in, ***174***
Fruit trees, ***129***
Fuchsias, ***51***

G

Garden compositions, 96–97
Garden habitats, 164–187
humid climates, 170–175
lofty elevations, 166–169
urban and desert oases, 184–187
wooded locales, 176–183
Gardenia, ***99***
Garden ornaments, theft of, 133
Garden pathways, 120–127
Garden rooms, ***26***, ***68***, 68–71
Garden sheds, 169
Garden styles
American regional, 54–63
historical American, 48–53
intentional, 34–46
Garlic 'Silver Lace', ***96***
Gas logs, 71
Gates, 111, ***116–117***
Gazanias, 187
'Sundrop', ***187***
Gazebos, ***12***, ***28***, ***51***, ***118***
screens in, 119
Genista lydia, ***148***
Geranium endressii 'Wargrave Pink', ***148***
Geraniums, ***31***
Globe lights, 92
Golden chain tree (*Laburnum*), ***63***
Goldenrain trees (*Koel reuteria paniculata*), ***194–195***
Goldenrod, 189
Golden chain trees (*Laburnum* x *watereri* 'Vossii'), ***151***
Grass, ***79***
Greene, Charles, 51
Greene, Henry, 51
Green roof, 169
Grill, ***75***
Grotto, ***73***
Ground covers, drought-tolerant, 187
Guardian Stone, ***45***

H

Hardscaping, 97
Harmony, 14–15
Heavenly bamboo (*Nandina domestica*), ***197***
Helichrysum italicum (curry plant), ***16***
Helonias bullata (swamp pinks), ***56***, ***171***
Herbs, ***70–71***
Hollyhocks, ***171***, ***176***
Honey locust 'Sunburst', ***99***
Honeysuckle, ***38***, ***99***
Horizontal breaks, 18
Hornbeam trees, ***69***, ***100***
Hosta albomarginata, ***99***
Hosta plantaginea, ***99***
Hostas, ***176***, ***181***
Humid climates, 170–175
Hydrangea, ***20***, ***99***

I

Ice plants (var. Delosperma), ***169***, 187
Ilex aquifolium 'Golden Queen', ***103***
Impatiens, ***31***, ***61***, ***166***, ***193***
Indoors, merging with outdoors, 161
Information, gathering, 24–27
Insect control, birds in, 163
International styles, 34–46
Chinese gardens, 35
English gardens, 36–37
French aesthetic gardens, 40
global influences, 34
Italian gardens, 42–43
Japanese gardens, 44–45
Persian gardens, 41
Spanish gardens, 46–47
Victorian gardens, 38–39
Zen minimalism gardens, 45
Ipomoea alba (moonvines), ***146***
Ironwork fences, ***115***
Italian gardens, ***34***, ***42–43***
Ivy, ***147***

J

Jacob's ladder, ***98***
Japanese anemone (*Anemone hupehensis* var. *japonica*), ***194***
'Bressingham Glow', ***194***
Japanese gardens, ***34***, ***44–45***, ***121***
Japanese maple trees, ***107***
Jefferson, Thomas, 149
Jekyll, Gertrude, 36, 53, 97
Joe-Pye weed, ***180***
Juniper, ***107***, ***166***
Juniperus sabina, ***45***
Juniperus virginiana (pencil cedars), ***15***

K

Knot gardens, 104–105
Koelreuteria paniculata (goldenrain trees), ***194–195***

L

Laburnum (golden chain tree), ***63***
Laburnum x watereri 'Vossii' (golden chain trees), ***151***
Landscape architects, 31

Index

Landscape contractors, 31
Landscape design, ***17***, 31
Landscape patterns, using, 19
Landscaping plan, 10–31
  devising your scheme, 28–31
  gathering information, 24–27
  principles of design, 12–23
Lanterns, ***92***
Lath, ***146–147***
  removable panels, 146
Lavender hedges, ***100***
Lawnmower storage, 145
Lawn substitutes, 187
Lennox-Boyd, Arabella, 142
Lettuce, ***104***, ***108***
Leucospermum cordifolium (pincushion protea), ***181***
Liatris, ***30***
Lighting, 17, 80–93
  appropriateness for plants, 27
  decorating with, 84–85
  developing scheme for, 88–90
  downlighting, 86, 87
  fairy lights, ***86–87***
  fixture options, 92
  floodlights, ***84***
  installing low-voltage, ***89***
  low-profile, ***84***
  making plan for, 88
  outdoor illumination, 82–87
  shopping for, 93
  spotlights, ***83***, ***84***
  underwater lights, ***83***, ***85***
  uplighting, 80–81, ***86***
Ligularia stenocephala 'The Rocket', ***171***
Limbed up trees, 166–167
Limestone sculptures, ***35***
Liriope, ***79***
Living walls and partitions, 100–101
Lobelia, ***51***
Lofty elevations, 166–169
Lotus, ***23***
Low-voltage lights, installing, ***89***
Lupines, ***62***, ***148***
Lutyens, Edwin, 36, 53
Lutyens bench, ***53***
Luzula nivea (white-flowering woodrush), ***98***

M

Mandevillas 'Red Riding Hood', ***175***
Marguerite daisy, ***99***
Marigolds, ***51***
Mass, 18
Master plan, need for cohesive, 11
Meadow, creating, 182–183
Measuring your property, 24, 25
Meidiland shrub rose 'Sevillana', ***114***
Microclimates, 167
Middleton Place Plantation, 152
Midwest garden, ***54***
Miscanthus sinensis 'Gracillimus' (ornamental grass), ***28***, ***55***, 189, ***194***
Monochromatic relationships, 23
Moonflowers, ***99***
Moon gardens, 99
Moon Stone, ***45***
Moonvines (*Ipomoea alba*), ***146***
Mortared stone retaining wall, ***183***
Mosaic pebble paving, ***20***
Moss, ***127***
Mulching mower, ***195***
Muscari (grape hyacinth), 126
Mushroom lights, ***92–93***

N

Nandina domestica (heavenly bamboo), ***197***
Naturalistic waterfall, ***29***
New Zealand flax (*Phormium tenax*), ***23***, ***94***, ***172***
Night jessamine, ***99***
Northeast garden, ***54***

O

Ogee arch, ***28***, ***144***
Ornamental grass (*Miscanthus sinensis* 'Gracillimus'), ***28***, ***55***, 189, ***194***
Ornaments, 132–133
Oryza sativai 'Red Dragon', ***128***
Outdoor fabrics, keeping clean, 157
Outdoor kitchen, planning, 75
Outdoor living space, 65–79
  defining your, 66–67
  dining in, 74–75
  family-friendly play areas, 72–73
  front gardens, 78–79
  garden rooms, 68–71
  secret retreats, 76–77
Outdoors, merging with indoors, 161
Outhouse, ***145***
Oxley, Mark, 85

P

Pachysandra, ***79***
Pacific Northwest garden, ***54***
Palm trees, ***166***, ***174***
Papaver rhoeas (Flanders poppies), 111
Parterres de broderie, ***40***
Patios, 155–161
  fireplaces for, ***71***
  flagstone, ***28***
  stone, ***112***
  Patterns
  shade, 27
  sun, 27
Paving stones, 161
Pencil cedars (*Juniperus virginiana*), ***15***
Pennisetum alopecuroides (fountain grass), ***166***, ***172***, ***180***
Pennsylvania bluestone, ***160***, ***161***
Perennial borders, 36
Pergola, ***50***, 112
  wisteria-covered, ***17***
Perilla frutescens, ***96***
Persian gardens, ***34***, ***41***
Persian shield, ***12***
Petunias, ***51***
Phillyrea angustifolia (false olive), ***104–105***
Phlox 'David', ***99***
Phlox divaricata (wild sweet William), ***56***, ***171***
Phormium tenax (New Zealand flax), ***94***, ***172***
Pieris japonica, ***176***, ***197***
Pincushion flower, ***98***
Pincushion protea (*Leucospermum cordifolium*), ***181***
Planting designs, 94–109
  charming topiaries as, 102–103
  color-themed gardens as, 98–99
  garden compositions as, 96–97
  knot gardens as, 104–105
  living walls and partitions as, 100–101
  plants for drama in, 106–107
  vegetable gardens as, 108–109
Plants for drama, 106–107
Plat map, ***25***
Play areas, family-friendly, ***72–73***
Playhouses, ***72***
Pleaching, ***151***
Plumbago (*Ceratopteris plumbaginoides*), ***56***
Polyethylene, 138
Polyvinyl chloride (PVC), 138
Ponds, ***18***
  flexible liners for, 138
  raised, ***29***, 169
  reflecting, ***70–71***
Potentilla, ***23***
Potting benches, ***144***
Prairie garden, ***55***, ***168***
Pressure-treated lumber, 154
Primroses, 56, ***138***, ***171***, ***181***
Primula florindae, ***171***
Private spa, ***76***
Problems, turning into assets, 132
Professional, hiring, 31
Proportion, 16
Pumpkins, ***109***
Purple basil, ***96***

Q

Quadrant gardens, ***49***
Quartzite flagstones, ***161***
Queen palms, ***107***

R

Railroad ties
  as retaining wall, ***166***
  as steps, ***167***
"Rainfall" waterfall, ***60***
Raised beds, ***185***

Raised fountain, ***29***
Raised pond, ***29***, ***169***
Red osier dogwood (*Cornus sericea*), ***176***
Redtwig dogwood (*Cornus alba* 'Sibirica'), ***197***
Red valerian (*Centranthus rubra*), ***148***
Reflecting pond, ***70–71***
Repetition, 15
Retaining walls, ***29***
of mortared stone, ***183***
of railroad ties, ***166***
Rhododendrons, ***62***, ***176***
River stones, ***161***
Robinson, William, 36, 48, 53
Rock gardens, ***39***, ***180***
Roof gardens, 166, ***168***
Roses, ***31***, ***37***, ***99***, ***123***
'Chris Evert', ***96***
red, ***123***
Rot-resistant woods, 154
Rudbeckia fulgida 'Goldsturm' (black-eyed susan), ***55***
Russian sage, ***180***

S

Salix helvetica (Swiss willow), ***101***
Saxifrage, ***181***
Scale, 16
Scilla campanulata (Spanish bluebells), ***191***
Screens, gazebo, 119
Sculptures, 111, 132–133
Seaside gardens, ***12***, 171, 172
Seasonal gardens, 189–197
autumn, 194–195
spring, 190–191
summer, 192–193
winter, 196–197
Secret retreats, ***77***
Sedum, ***169***, 187
'Autumn Joy', ***12***, 189
'Dragon's Blood', ***123***
Seed heads, ***194***
Serpentine walls, 148, ***149***
Shade-loving shrubs, ***176***
Shade patterns, 27
Shade trees, ***76***
Shadows, 17
Shady garden, ***185***
Sidalcia, ***171***
Silver lamb's ears, ***96***, ***101***
Site map, 24, 26
Sites, analysis of, 24–27
Slope, terraced, 153
Sloped fences, 114–117, ***115***
Smoke tree (*Cotinus coggyria purpureau*), ***23***
Snowdrops, ***190***
Softscaping, 97
Sorbia aria (whitebeam), ***118***
South garden, ***54***
Southwest garden, ***54***
Space, 18
defining, 66–67
Spanish bluebells (*Scilla campanulata*), ***191***
Spanish gardens, ***34***, ***46–47***
Split-rail fences, ***114***
Spotlights, 92, ***93***
Spring gardens, 190–191
Spring meadows, 183
Spruce, ***23***
Square flagstones, ***122***
Stairs, stone, ***124***
Stepped fence, 114
Stepping-stone path, ***96***, ***179***
Steps, railroad ties as, ***167***
Stone bench, ***157***
Stone patios, ***112***
Stone slabs, ***78***
Stone stairs, ***79***, ***124***
Stone walls, ***148***
Storage, lawnmower, 145
Straw bee skeps, ***49***
Strawberry pots, ***129***
Strelitzia nicolai (bird of paradise), ***97***
Stylized leaf chair, ***157***
Submersible mist fogger, ***139***
Succulents, ***61***, ***169***, ***184–185***, ***187***
Summer gardens, 192–193
Summer meadows, 183
Sundials, ***134–135***
setting time on, 135
Sun patterns, 27
Sun/shade log, 27
Surface deck lights, 92
Suspension bridge, ***77***
Swamp pinks (*Helonias bullata*), ***56***, ***171***
Sweet alyssum, ***97***
Sweet peas, ***99***
Sweet-potato vine 'Blackie', ***12***
Swimming pools, ***15***, ***140–141***
equipment for, ***145***
Swings, ***72***
Swiss willow (*Salix helvetica*), ***101***
Symmetry, 57, ***57***
Synthetic-rubber sheeting, 138

T

Tennessee sandstone, ***161***
Terraced slope, 153
Terraces, ***152–153***
Terra-cotta tile paving, ***161***
Terrazzo, ***160***
Textures, using, for visual variety, 20
Theft of garden ornaments, 133
'Tiger Eye' sumac, ***20***
Tiled walkway, ***79***
Time, setting right, 135
Ting (pavilion), ***35***
Toll, Julie, 118
Topiaries, 102–103
Trellised vines, ***185***
Trellises, ***74***, ***146–147***
Triad relationships, 23
Trompe l'oeil, ***149***
Tropical gardens, ***174–175***
Tulip poplar trees, ***127***
Tulips, ***13***, ***191***

U

Underplantings, ***96***
Unity, 14–15
Uplighting, well-placed, 80–81
Urban oases, 184–187

V

Valerian, ***148***
Variegated ivy, ***102***
Vegetable gardens, 108–109
Verbascum, ***13***
Verbena, ***12***
Vermont slate, ***161***
Victorian gardens, ***38–39***, 48, 50
Vista, ***26***
Visual variety, using texture for, 20

W

Walkways, 111
Waterfalls, 111, ***142–143***, ***181***
Water features, 136–144, ***193***
Watering, absentee, 192
Water lilies, ***99***, ***143***
Wattle fence, ***49***
Wax begonias, ***51***, ***59***, ***193***
Well lights, 92
Whitebeam (*Sorbia aria*), ***118***
White-flowering woodrush (*Luzula nivea*), ***98***
Wicker-and-rattan chairs, ***156***
Wild columbine (*Aquilegia canadensis*), ***191***
Wildflower meadow, ***62***, 183
Wild sweet William (*Phlox divaricata*), ***56***, ***171***
Window boxes, ***72***
Winter gardens, 196–197
Wish list, 29
Wisteria-covered pergola, ***17***
Witch hazel 'Primavera', ***196***
Wood chips, ***30***
Wooded locales, 176–183
Wood options, 154
Wrought iron, ***57***

Y

Yellow-colored lights, 84
Yellow yarrow, ***22***
Yews, ***67***, ***102***
Yucca, ***59***
Yucca filamentosa, ***166***
Yukimi-gata (snow viewing) lantern, ***45***

Z

Zen minimalism, 45
Zinnia 'Zowie', ***162***